We'll Always
Have Cleveland

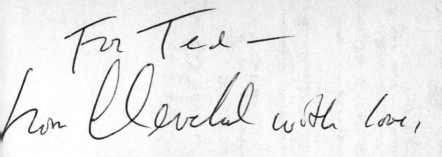

For Ted —
from Cleveland with love,

We'll Always Have Cleveland

A Memoir of a Novelist and a City

Les Roberts

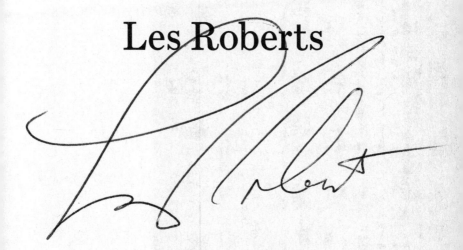

GRAY & COMPANY, PUBLISHERS
CLEVELAND

Gray & Company, Publishers
www.grayco.com

ISBN-13: 978-1-59851-014-0
ISBN-10: 1-59851-014-2
Printed in the United States of America
First printing

This book is dedicated to all the people I love—even the ones I might have forgotten to mention here—but especially to those I love best in all the world: my daughter Valerie; my son Darren; my granddaughter Shea; and the beautiful and amazing woman who makes my sun shine and my stars twinkle, Holly Albin.
Thank you all for everything.

Contents

Introduction   1

1. I Barely Ever Heard of Cleveland   6

2. A Dentist in Parma   19

3. A Little Old Man in Jersey   28

4. Watch Out!   36

5. All Around Town   48

6. "You're a Strange Person"   68

7. Milan and Me   88

8. "Here's to Us. Who's Like Us? Damn Few"   99

9. A Little Glitch   118

10. One Man's Poison   137

11. Food, Glorious Food!   146

12. When You Haven't Got Your Gun   157

13. Bones to Pick   172

We'll Always
Have Cleveland

Introduction

I'M A WRITER. That's what I do. I've done other things, too, in my life, but there wasn't a single day that part of me wasn't writing. Something.

In 1988, I published a mystery novel, *Pepper Pike*, about a private investigator from Cleveland named Milan Jacovich. I couldn't have known it at the time, but that book was the start of a thirteen-book series that would lead me to Cleveland—and also introduce my adopted hometown to many mystery fans all over the country.

I've completed so many novels and short stories set in and around the city in the past fifteen years or so that Clevelanders assume I'm a born-and-bred native. In fact, most people ask, "What made you come *back* to Cleveland?" as if they can't believe anyone in their right mind would voluntarily leave the endless sunshine and the glitz and glitter of Southern California where I lived for nearly a quarter of a century to return to a gritty, blue-collar, bad-weather place like Cleveland.

The truth is that I came to my adopted city fairly late in my life, and learned to love and respect it for all that it was and all that I saw it could be. In the first part of my adult life I wrote mostly scripts, articles, letters, television shows, game shows, comedy sketches, and even satirical songs. It was a career that began in Chicago, followed me to New York City, and then west for a long and sometimes crazy stay in Los Angeles.

Way back in the dawning era of technology, I pounded everything out on an IBM Selectric. Since 1986, when I exchanged my typewriter for a basic computer, I've mostly written books, and that has been the best and most fun part of all. Better yet, beginning in late 1990 I started writing all those books here in Cleveland.

This book is my story. But it is not an autobiography. Although I think my pre-Cleveland years were very interesting, they were interesting only to *me*. Besides, unless they are Winston Churchill or Laurence Olivier, I find people who write autobiographies guilty of the most astonishing hubris. I'm sure nobody cares about my sixth-grade teacher's name, or even with whom I shared my first kiss. (Come to think of it, I don't recall her name, either.)

Autobiographies are too damned intimate, too. I love chatting with everyone, strangers as well as friends, but the fact is that I'm really a very private person. If I ever feel the need to expose the darkest secrets of my life—and you can take a deep breath and hold it waiting for *that* to happen—I'll write it as a novel instead, changing all the character names (to protect the innocent and not-so-innocent), and nobody will ever realize the lead character is me. That's the joy of writing fiction: you can sometimes tell the whole truth, but readers never know whether or not to believe it.

Most people know, from my book jackets, that I was born in Chicago. I married young, I had two children, I divorced.

I had some fun times in Hollywood, where I produced and wrote for television programs, mostly game shows, bristling with the illustrious names of show business. (Who wouldn't, in their mid-twenties, deny having fun sitting at a large table in the now-gone Chasen's, the fabled Beverly Hills eatery that served the most delicious chili I'd ever tasted, and swapping jokes and one-liners with comic legends like Milton Berle, Steve Allen, and Buddy Hackett?)

I met a lot of truly interesting people, some of whom were

famous. I worked with many, socialized with some, and dated a few. And, working in Hollywood, you never knew who you'd bump into.

I literally ran into Joe DiMaggio turning a corner inside a studio (and I'm thankful I had enough presence of mind to call him "*Mister* DiMaggio" because when he died I read that he'd resented fans' overfamiliarity in calling him "Joe").

I once smiled at Jimmy Stewart in a crowded elevator when nobody else recognized him in his floppy old fishing hat, and he shook his head very slightly at me so I wouldn't say anything to him and make everyone else in the elevator turn and begin bothering him or asking for autographs. When we reached the main floor, as he walked past me out the door he gave me a playful poke and a wink, but we never did speak. I *did* get the opportunity to say a quiet good morning to Oscar winner Ray Milland at a coffeehouse down in Redondo Beach. Everyone else who was majorly famous I left alone unless we were working together or we'd been formally introduced.

Another time, I went into the makeup room at NBC in Burbank one early evening, and saw an elderly man sitting in the makeup chair, all covered from the neck down with a protective smock. Rather somberly, he said "Good evening" and I greeted him with a breezy "Hiya." Then he rose from the chair, the makeup apron fell away, and I saw the well-tailored uniform with the gold braid and those *five* silver stars on his shoulder and realized I'd just said "Hiya" to General of the Army Omar Bradley. I was nearly tongue-tied. Needless to say, I apologized profusely for not recognizing him earlier; the general was gracious and polite. He asked me what my job was, and when I proudly announced I was the producer of *The Hollywood Squares*, he looked at me blankly and said, "What are they?"

It was one of many moments of budding wisdom, when my

self-importance bubble was punctured and I got a true picture of where I stood in the great scheme of things. He was the most exalted American hero still alive, and had almost literally saved the world with his leadership and strategy during World War II; I was the producer of a daytime game show. I figured out quickly which of us was really somebody. I'd recommend such a learning experience to anyone who happens to think he or she's pretty hot stuff.

Often it's been suggested that I write a memoir of my years in Hollywood. Frankly, all those days are a distant memory to me now. All the so-called stars with whom I interacted are either dead, or they haven't made a film or a TV show in twenty years. Besides, the most anyone ever wants to hear about those Hollywood times now is "What was Paul Newman really like?" (I met Paul Newman once for about ninety seconds back around 1970, and other than wishing I looked half as good as he did—a wish I still haven't abandoned even though he is now in his eighties and I still look only half as good as he does—I haven't the foggiest notion of what he's like. At the time, I had no clue he was from Shaker Heights—and I wasn't so sure what and where Shaker Heights was, either.)

I had a lot of laughs in those years—until I realized I was laughing *at* the Hollywoodies and not with them. Being a born Chicagoan, I had a much different moral compass, a middle-western value system, than did many of my show business compadres; and while I did enough unforgivable garbage to last me more than two lifetimes out there, I really only stayed because if one wanted to be connected with movies or television, Los Angeles was where the work was—and still is.

Since I moved to Northeast Ohio, Greater Cleveland has inspired and nurtured and fostered me—and on more than one occasion pissed me off—clearly stamping my writing style and greatly influencing the person I have become. Since moving here, I've become a dyed-in-the-wool Clevelander, with more shirts and jackets than I can count bearing the logos and colors of the Indians or the Browns, and team flags proudly displayed in the back window of my car during the appropriate seasons.

It's perceived that I know more about Cleveland than most natives do, but that's because I run around with a notebook or a tape recorder all the time recording my impressions of the city, or perfect strangers come up to talk to me and tell me wonderful local lore that often winds up in one of my books. I know that Moses Cleaveland spelled his name wrong and that Mayor Ralph Perk's wife turned down an invitation to the Nixon White House so she wouldn't miss her bowling night, but mostly I ignore local history. I'm hardly a Cleveland scholar, nor am I in any way a historian. I write fiction—entertainment, or at least I hope that's what it is—and while I outsell many more famous authors, at least in this area, I'm every bit as thrilled to find out someone in Walla Walla, Washington, is reading my work as someone who lives across the street.

Ever since I moved here I've been enjoying every moment, sucking up everything I can about my adoptive city, letting it permeate my imagination and my fiction, and figuring out a way to put it all on paper in one book or another so I can share it with everyone.

This book is the story of how I came to know the city through the eyes of a fictional character, one that I created out of whole cloth. It's a kind of Cleveland memoir—of me, of a lot of the people I care about, of a fictional Slovenian-American private investigator named Milan Jacovich, of the writing process, and of the city and region itself.

CHAPTER 1

I Barely Ever Heard of Cleveland

EACH TIME I'VE sat down to begin a new novel, I've always thought of my first three months in Cleveland, and remembered what captivated me, made me move here, and inspired me to write thirteen books and countless short stories about a city that is too often like Rodney Dangerfield—it don't get no respect.

When I first arrived here in January of 1987, I was a complete Cleveland virgin. Born and raised in Chicago back in the day when my parents didn't own a car and taking a three-state jaunt over the weekend just for fun was unthinkable, and living all my adult life in New York and then Los Angeles—with a couple of time-outs in Georgia, courtesy of the United States Army, and in Hong Kong to write a very bad film project that some twenty-five years later turned into a novel—all I knew about Cleveland was Bob Feller, Jim Brown, and the Cuyahoga River catching fire.

I'd heard all the Cleveland jokes perpetuated by television's Johnny Carson and his Cleveland native-son head writer, the late Pat McCormick, when they finally tired of poking fun at Pittsburgh. However, I was laughing over something I knew virtually nothing about. I was vaguely aware that there was a Great Lake up here somewhere. I knew it wasn't Lake Michigan because that body of water was the eastern border of Chicago and I had spent my childhood in a seventh-floor apartment looking out on the waves crashing against the rocks of that lake, so I figured out the big body of water just north of this city is Lake Erie. Otherwise, I'd barely ever heard of Cleveland.

When I accepted a job at Marcus Advertising to come here for three months to conceptualize, create, and get on its feet a weekly television game show for the Ohio Lottery—a show called *Cash Explosion* which, eighteen years later is still on the air, albeit in a slightly different form, and which hasn't paid me a nickel's worth of money since 1987—I had to ask exactly what everyone *did* in Cleveland. At that time I had no knowledge of the Northeast Ohio steel industry, about which I've since written with such affection, nor the immigrant culture that the steel business spawned. I knew Detroit made cars and Pittsburgh was a steel town, but I hadn't a clue as to what economic engine floated the boats on the North Coast.

In fact, I didn't know it was called the North Coast until I got off the plane and saw the sign in the Cleveland Hopkins Airport, welcoming travelers.

I arrived in the evening on the first Sunday in January of 1987, and I'm sure it will surprise no one that it was snowing, because that's generally what it always does in a cold Cleveland January. I'd seen my share of snow as a child in Chicago—which probably doesn't get as much snowfall in any given year as Cleveland does, but I was younger. I was a lot shorter then, too, and it *seemed* like a lot of snow. After more than two decades living in Los Angeles, the gently falling flakes that landed in my hair and on my eyelashes on that January Sunday were the first of many things that made me think I might learn to love Cleveland.

It didn't even matter that, because in Southern California it never drops below fifty degrees, all I'd brought with me in the way of outerwear was a flimsy trench coat with a removable lining that would prove as effective at keeping at bay the blizzards of a Cleveland winter as a flashlight would be in illuminating the Grand Canyon at night.

Nevertheless, I'd been working in network and syndicated television for too long, and was thrilled to be getting out of la-la land long enough to get acclimated somewhere else for the first time in more than twenty years. I needed a chance to experience how the rest of the country—the *real* people, not the show business egomaniacs—lived.

I was picked up at the airport and driven across town to a hotel in Beachwood—just a few blocks from the offices of Marcus Advertising—until more suitable accommodations could be found. As we crossed the Main Avenue Bridge, I looked out across the Flats at downtown and the Terminal Tower, all lit up and glistening through the falling snow. The scene was so warm and welcoming that it occurred to me I might like this new city very much.

I had no idea how much it would eventually get under my skin and into my bloodstream. There are those who smoke one cigarette, drink one drink, or try a sample of one drug and they are hooked from the beginning. Cleveland hooked me, beginning that very first night.

It's a city that has steadily fired my writer's imagination, a place I've grown more and more crazy about with every passing month (despite all its warts and wens)—a destination in which I have really felt a part of the community. I've learned an awful lot about the city and region, and the wonderful and sometimes maddening people who live here. I know the area very well now, although I'm still learning—east to Warren, south to Holmes County, west to Elyria, and of course every inch of downtown and the Flats and Tremont and Ohio City, and every street in Cleveland Heights and Shaker Heights.

I've lived here for a decade and a half now, but I still can't drive downtown or across the river to the West Side without feeling a little lump of pride in my chest as I think, "This is *my* town." It really is, too.

Cleveland is a major-league city with major-league sports, a huge fan base for arts and culture, and a diversity of citizens whose backgrounds cover almost a hundred different ethnicities. Unlike Los Angeles, where I could live for ten years and never have the opportunity to speak to my next-door neighbor, Cleveland and its suburbs are a busy maze where everyone seems to know everyone else.

For all its big-city perks and activities and attractions— and scandals, too—Cleveland is a small town, or at least a medium-sized one broken up into many small neighborhoods. I hardly ever go out of the house, especially in Cleveland Heights and Shaker Heights and of course Cleveland itself, when I don't run into somebody I know.

Living here for so long that I now think of myself as a Clevelander, it tickles me to remember back to that first week, when I went into raptures at seeing my first frozen pond in twenty-one years, when I was forced to go out and buy a pair of rubber overshoes to protect my flimsy California shoes from nearly a foot of slush, or how amused I was after I'd put in a full day at work and came outside at five o'clock to see everyone who worked in my building at Landmark Centre chipping ice off the windshields of their cars, their breaths freezing in a puff of smoke and their noses turning red with the cold. Then realized I'd soon be driving a rental car—and having to chip away at my the ice on my own windshield.

It was an actual *season*, like the kind I'd grown up with in Chicago. There would be four of them! Summer heat would give way to the cool, snappy breezes of autumn, then to cold and snowy December through March, and then to warm and green spring again.

I'd grown bored with the unchanging seasons during

my California years. In Los Angeles, it's summer for eleven months, followed by heavy cold rains in February, and then the cycle begins again. I actually found myself relishing the bad weather on the shores of Lake Erie as I drove around and looked at the sights, the old and interesting architecture, and the people who lived here and dressed up in protective clothing—virtually everyone here wears a parka, most with interesting color combinations.

When I submitted *The Lake Effect* to my agent, who lives in New York, he observed that my first four books in the Milan series all had something about Cleveland in the title and this one should, too. I had to point out that everyone in Northeast Ohio *knows* that anything called *The Lake Effect* has something to do with them. That's because we all listen to the weather reports each night; it would be crazy not to. I'm not sure New Yorkers have ever heard of the lake effect. I know I hadn't, in Manhattan or in Los Angeles, either, until I moved to Cleveland. All these years later, I still enjoy the winter—but I have to admit I don't have to go out in it every day, either. I enjoy looking at it, though, through the windows on three sides of the second-floor sunroom in which I spend most of my day, writing.

When I actually moved to Cleveland back in the winter of 1990, I'd driven all the way from California with not much in my old car except three days' worth of clothes (I stopped at my daughter's house in Denver and got them washed) and, of course, my computer. I was passing through Columbus, Ohio, looking forward to taking possession of my house the next morning, and as I fiddled with the radio dial I somehow heard a broadcast originating in Cleveland that informed me that there was currently an area blizzard and an ice storm on Cedar Hill—the only way I knew (at the time) how to get to Cleveland Heights from downtown—and that driving was particularly hazardous. After spending a generation in Los Angeles, that weather report gave me a chill that had nothing to do with the winter temperature.

I found out the next morning, when I finally arrived, that the "blizzard" had not been a problem at all. While it can snow like murder here, the very next day the white ground cover often begins melting away.

What truly struck me about that initial week in Cleveland in 1987, beyond the exhilarating weather and the beautiful architecture and the friendliness of the people, was Browns Mania. I wasn't a huge football fan during my Southern California stay, even though, like everyone else, I perked up during the Super Bowl; baseball was more my game, specifically the Los Angeles Dodgers. But in the 1986 season, quarterback Bernie Kosar and coach Marty Schottenheimer had led their team to the playoffs for the first time in decades, and when I got here—the evening after they'd won their first postseason game (over the New York Jets)—the whole city was agog with excitement.

That was a change for me as well. In Southern California, when the Dodgers or the Rams or the Lakers won a championship, only half the local citizenry even knew about it, and only five percent of them actually cared one way or the other—more than enough to fill the stadiums, of course, in a community of fourteen million people. Still, there was little civic boosterism for sports in Los Angeles, or, frankly, much of anything else except movies and TV. It's a city where the population lives and dies on the box office success of their last picture or the ratings of their most recent TV show and doesn't much worry about such trivia as sports.

In Cleveland, the Browns are everybody's business. Every time we trade a player or hire a new coach, there's nobody within a hundred-mile radius of Public Square who doesn't have an opinion about it one way or the other, a wise and learned opinion they are more than happy to share.

The day before the playoff game against the Denver Broncos—the one that would be played in a blizzard forever known as "Ice Station Cleveland"—came six days after I arrived in Cleveland. It was a Saturday, and I had stopped into a little delicatessen in Shaker Heights to order a takeout lunch. Standing in line directly in front of me were two elderly Jewish ladies, both in their eighties or perhaps even older. The taller of them was probably four feet eleven inches, and both were adorable all wrapped up in their cold-weather gear so that only their eyes and noses showed. They looked around the deli at the walls plastered with Browns stuff—orange pompons and banners, posters of Bernie Kosar and Ozzie Newsome, and panoramic views of the now-gone Cleveland Municipal Stadium. One lady turned to the other and said fervently, "Oy, that Bernie! Is he wonderful? Could he throw that ball! I love that Bernie!"

My love affair with the city began that frosty Saturday, and many years later with a closet full of Browns and Indians shirts and jackets, that civic lust burns as hot as ever.

I received another real tug at my heartstrings that same week when I visited another store and on the wall was a poster of the rival quarterback, Denver's John Elway, hung upside down like some sort of icon in a satanic ritual, with an X drawn across his face with a thick Magic Marker. Clevelanders showed that they were not only fiercely loyal to their team, but had a sense of humor about it, too.

They don't have much of a sense of humor about the Pittsburgh Steelers, though—or, about the Baltimore Ravens and former Browns owner Art Modell. When the Cleveland football team returned to the NFL after a long absence in the late 1990s, one of my California friends, mystery novelist and football fanatic Gar Anthony Haywood, asked me if the Browns would have the same kind of rivalry with Baltimore as they did with Pittsburgh. I had to reply, "With the Steelers it's a rivalry; with Art Modell's Ravens, it's a *jihad.*"

Along with most Cleveland-area sports fanatics, I am still angry with the Baltimore Ravens. When my son, Darren, introduced me to the beautiful young woman named Anne Kelley whom he ultimately married on a beach in Maui, he told me she was a Baltimore native now living in Los Angeles. I grew to love her only after she assured me that she and her family members were not Ravens boosters.

The Browns, by the way, lost that 1987 playoff game to the Broncos. It would be a better story if they'd won, then gone on to capture the Super Bowl, coinciding with my first visit here—but there I go, writing fiction again.

• • •

IT WAS A perfect time for me to explore a new city and a new rhythm of life. I was at a transition point in early 1987, both in my career and in my love life. I was in the throes of ending a long-term romantic relationship, and after years of writing and producing network and syndicated television—which is why Marcus Advertising and the Ohio Lottery asked me to come to Cleveland to create their game show in the first place—I had just completed and sold my first novel, *An Infinite Number of Monkeys*, featuring a Los Angeles private investigator named Saxon. It won an award as the Best First Private Eye Novel of 1987, and I was nearly finished writing a follow-up, which I planned to complete in the evenings after my work at Marcus was done. I had every reason to believe I wouldn't have to go back to the network grind again; I had hated it for all the years I lived in Hollywood.

There is no pressure I can imagine like the responsibility of churning out five television programs every week. For twenty-four years I was a producer and writer in Los Angeles, and I have to assure you that anyone who is a producer and insists that he is a completely nice guy is probably either a former producer, a never-was producer, or a liar. Most of them, unlike physicians who go to med school and lawyers who pass the bar exam, simply drop into the nearest Kinko's and have business cards printed up announcing they are a producer. At least half the strange people you'll meet on the streets in Hollywood and on Sunset Strip have business cards like that, and they're all full of crap.

I felt that writing a book was *real* writing, not penning a script that was then picked over and altered by a minimum of fifteen different studio executives and network "suits." Coming to Cleveland was a chance for me to regroup and to straighten out my own head and decide what I wanted to do with the rest of my life.

That initial three months went by too quickly. I recall one Sunday morning when, after six weeks of bitter cold and wet, biting weather, I awoke to find the temperature in Cleveland hovering around seventy degrees and the sun shining brightly. I couldn't wait to get out of the house and do something. I saw several convertibles with their canvas tops pulled down, and several people on the street were wearing shorts and T-shirts. I wound up spending the day at the Metroparks Zoo without an overcoat, thinking that the balmy temperatures matched those where I lived, Los Angeles. Disappointment set in the next morning when the temperature dipped about forty degrees and it was chilly winter once again.

What amazed me the most was how Clevelanders are so warm and cordial. In L.A., kindness from strangers is immediately viewed with suspicion and hostility, and the first reaction is to grope for one's wallet to make sure it's still there. In the aggressive and highly suspect city of Los Angeles, chances are the wallet *will* be spirited away—along with the pants in which you kept it. Northeast Ohio was totally different, from the beginning.

The people I worked closely with here—account executive Jim Reed, production supervisor Bud Ford, and producer Rick Alexander—were remarkably kind to me, as were David Gale and Anne Bloomberg of the Lottery, and of course Don Marcus, who has since passed on. When I first met him he was well into his seventies and able to run a big advertising agency without losing his head or his sense of humor. Jim and Eileen Terry-Reed's lovely estate in Gates Mills and Rick and Betsy Alexander's hilltop house in Lakewood became second homes to me, and virtually everyone I met, knowing I was a stranger in town, made sure that I always had something interesting and fun to do on weekends or in the evening.

In *Pepper Pike*, I wrote about the imagined goings-on in an advertising agency similar to Marcus Advertising. The murder victim was an account executive—venal, ambitious, a serial womanizer, and a compulsive gambler—and my friend Jim Reed is to this day convinced the fictional victim was fashioned in his image, despite the fact that he is the kindest, gentlest man I've ever met, adores his wife Eileen, and as far as I know gambles on nothing more sinister than a weekly lottery ticket. The only similarity between the two, to which I'll readily admit, is that they both like to write nearly everything with a brown felt-tip pen.

Often after work I'd stop at Nighttown and have a drink with brand-new Cleveland friends—like Marji Dodrill, who worked at Marcus and was vital in helping us do run-throughs of the *Cash Explosion* show in the office to make sure the game worked. She was one of the best actresses I've ever met, and after I settled here three years later I saw her onstage many times in such plays as *Driving Miss Daisy*, *Medea*, and *The Perfect Ganesh*. We remained friends until she eventually lost the toughest and bravest fight I've ever seen anyone wage against cancer. She was my personal hero, and I was flattered and moved that her husband, Everett, asked me to be one of many speakers at her memorial service. (By the way, the Dodrill house and the Alexander house were used as settings in my future novels. In my first Cleveland book, *Pepper Pike*, my descriptions of my detective hero's former home, the one in which his ex-wife still lives, is reminiscent of Marj and Everett's place in Cleveland Heights. And the place where the first dead body is discovered in *Full Cleveland* is a dead ringer for where Rick and Betsy Alexander used to live in Lakewood.)

The Alexanders moved to New York, and the Reeds—with whom I shared every Christmas dinner and every Easter egg hunt on their back acres after I settled here, and to whom I dedicated one of my Milan Jacovich books—retired to Rehoboth Beach, Delaware and built a house not too far from the Atlantic Ocean. I miss them still, every day.

Part of my agreement with Marcus for creating the TV show was that I'd have a week off to go back to California midway during my stay. Since nothing in Los Angeles demanded my immediate attention—my children were more or less grown by then, and a friend was subletting my apartment—I chose to go to New York instead, where I looked up some old acquaintances. I had lived in Manhattan for ten years back in the middle of the last century, hanging out in drugstores or in the Automat diner with some people who later went on to deserved obscurity and others who eventually became household names in the theater, movies, and literary circles. During that week-long visit in 1987, I spent a leisurely and very wet lunch with my editor at St. Martin's Press, Tom Dunne. Dunne is a big, hearty Irishman and his editorial lunches were legendary; after nearly five hours of martinis and cognac, I frankly have little memory of getting back to my hotel. But before it got too drunk out, Tom suggested I start writing another mystery series, which I could alternate with the Saxon books.

"But don't set it in Los Angeles, because you're already doing one there," he said. "And don't set it in San Francisco or Boston or Chicago or New York, because they all have fictional private eyes, too."

I was frustrated; he'd just named every major city I'd ever visited in my life.

Except Cleveland.

When I suggested setting a series on the North Coast, he became very excited. At that time no one used Northeast Ohio as a base for mysteries except Max Allan Collins with his occasional Elliot Ness books, and they were all "period" mysteries, set in the thirties. There was no strong literary representation of present-day Cleveland, and Dunne wanted me to be the groundbreaker.

I was excited and a little awed by the challenge of creating another series so quickly, even though Saxon and I—then and now he doesn't have a first name—were still in the process of getting to know one another. But I was younger then, more naive, and disgustingly self-confident, so I began thinking of plots even before I left New York. All I really knew of Cleveland after only five weeks in residence was advertising agencies, so my thoughts drifted in that direction, and I filled several yellow pages with random scribbles and doodles as I drove around, talked to the new friends I'd made, and tried to figure out what there *was* about this town that I could capture and write about.

I was still missing the most vital ingredient for my new series of novels—the protagonist. I'd already decided he was going to be a tough guy private eye, tougher than Saxon. But that's virtually all I knew about the Cleveland private investigator whom I would create—not nearly enough to start writing a book. I understood that when I returned to Cleveland from New York I'd have to get busy, make some definite notes and perhaps ask some real questions, and at the least do some heavy research so I could create the kind of hero I wanted.

I'd planned on coming back on Sunday afternoon, but decided to visit the Metropolitan Museum of Art before I left New York (when I lived in Manhattan in my early adulthood, I went to the Museum once a month). I changed my reservation to an evening flight—that was back when they let you do things like that, before the Patriot Act and the impossibility of changing a flight at the last minute. I boarded the plane to return to Cleveland at approximately eight o'clock.

On such whimsical decisions does history often turn. Mine sure did.

CHAPTER 2

A Dentist in Parma

AFTER MY 1987 trip to New York and my promise to Tom Dunne to create a private eye series based here, I returned to Cleveland and my work on the *Cash Explosion* show. During my nonworking moments I put into motion a technique I like to call the "Writer's Eye." (You can call it the "Artist's Eye" or the "Actor's Eye" as well, because every creative artist walks around all the time recording in their mind the sights and sounds and images that may or may not be used some day in their work.) I began noting things about Cleveland that were unique, things I knew I'd have to include if the proposed series was to be real and believable.

What I discovered, of course, is that this is unlike any other city I've ever visited. I've been to plenty of towns and cities in America, and I've enjoyed most of them. Cleveland, especially, presented me with a veritable feast of delicious tales and legends and surprising truths, with some of the most startling early twentieth century American architecture anywhere. Progress, the bitch goddess, must be served, and the pitiless wrecking ball swings in Cleveland as often as anywhere else, but we've managed to retain many of our great buildings and historical statues, so our downtown is different from almost any other big city.

I learned something else when I'd been here less than a year, something I think about often. I was out to dinner with a friend one winter night, and she asked if I had ever visited the Flats, down by the river. I said that of course I had, but she corrected me. "You've never been in the belly of the Flats—never seen the industry close-up."

Then she directed me to drive into the part of the Flats I'd never seen before where large ore boats were discharging their cargo of coke—that's a fuel for making steel, not a drug—and where the factories were so huge, swathed with metal stairways and platforms, that they exuded a weird sense of mystery, and even danger. Their machines were so powerful that I could actually feel the ground shaking beneath my feet as we stood outside the car and watched.

I felt something industrial, rough-voiced and sweaty, that I'd never really noticed before. Not wanting to turn away and drive back to someplace grassy and pleasant in the city, I was awed—overcome with the "terrible beauty" of those buildings and machines that worked while the rest of the city slept. I've written about them a few times since.

It didn't take me long to realize that to give a novel a real Cleveland "feel," an author must either strongly consider for its protagonist the African-American community or the Eastern European one. At the time—and this was before Walter Mosley and Gar Anthony Haywood came along to write about their great black private eyes—there wasn't much of an African-American presence in mystery novels, even though in my second novel, *Not Enough Horses*, Saxon adopts a black street kid named Marvel. I was sorely tempted to create a tough and honest black man from Cleveland. But after thinking it over, I came to believe no Caucasian author can honestly capture the black experience in America, no matter how hard he tries. So I decided instead to make my series hero the descendant of an Eastern European family—either Serbian, Croatian, Hungarian, Lithuanian, or Slovenian.

But which? I began haunting the neighborhoods and the libraries in my spare time, reading everything I could, trying to make the right decision.

One single quote made the difference, and I can't even remember where I read it. It came from an article that said Serbians are astonishing fighters—so if you put three Serbs in a room together, you get a regiment. Three Croatians make a parliament—more likely to argue than to fight. But if you put three Slovenians together, you'll wind up with a chorus, because they love to sing. Since I was beginning to envision this yet-unnamed private eye as a gentle giant, a large man with an immigrant background, a football history, a Vietnam résumé, a few years on the police force, two little boys, and a divorced wife who had broken his heart, I decided I wanted my guy to be the less argumentative and more easygoing Slovenian.

In thirteen books, however, I never had him sing.

Now, I had to find out all about Slovenians, a subject of which I was totally ignorant. At the time I wasn't really sure where Slovenia was, or what the people who came from there were like. While there were plenty of books about the history and culture of the country, there was virtually nothing in print that fully explained the Slovenian experience in America.

Here's where I ran into another example of warm Cleveland hospitality and thoughtfulness, someone who generously got me started on the first of what would eventually be thirteen books.

The associate producer on *Cash Explosion* was Chris Sywyj (you non-Clevelanders can pronounce that "Sivvy"), who was working with us during our preproduction phase before she left to have her very imminent baby. Her husband is Dick Russ of Channel 3 News. Dick is the son of Slovenian immigrants, and even though he'd never met me, Chris told him of my interest in his ethnic heritage and he was kind enough to send me six single-spaced typewritten pages about the Slovenians of Cleveland—marvelous, evocative, usable stuff describing what they ate, how they dressed, their family dynamics, their financial habits and even their dating proclivities. One of my favorites that Dick Russ scribbled down for me was, "When a Slovenian man takes his date out for dinner in the evening, she can order anything on the menu she likes—but he's going to stick with the $7.95 pasta plate."

That absolutely described the Slovenian dating ethic, and I used it in one of the books.

I still have those six pages from Dick Russ, and they're nearly falling apart from use—I've never written a Milan Jacovich novel without consulting them heavily. I especially thank Dick for inspiring Milan's Auntie Branka in the first novel, created specifically from his notes—an elderly black-clad widow living in the east side suburb of Euclid, on whose stove something was always simmering, and who greets her nephew's phone call with "Milan! You don't call me for a month! Vatsa matter? You die or sometink?"

I only used Auntie Branka in that one book, *Pepper Pike*, but she is still the character most strangers want to talk about. Everyone, of every race and heritage, has or had an aunt or a grandmother or a mother like that, because like it or not, we are all the children of immigrants, and those wise, impatient, elderly women from another era and often another country, were and are a large part of who we've all become.

That was, of course, before I ever knew there was a "Milan." And specifically how he came about goes back once more to that three-day trip to New York—or rather, the trip home to Cleveland.

It was cold and snowy that night, and I found myself on the westbound plane sitting next to an attractive, pleasant young woman named Diana Montagino, who was more than a little nervous about flying in such bad weather. I joked with her to make her feel more relaxed, squeezed her hand during takeoff, and we passed a pleasant ninety minutes in the air, during which time I explained to her that I was only in Cleveland temporarily, producing a television show, and that I didn't know many people in town. I invited her to have lunch with me sometime.

We didn't get around to that lunch for more than two weeks, and I'm embarrassed to admit I don't remember where we ate. At a certain age, the memory starts to go, which is *another* reason I'll never write an autobiography. There are a lot of people in my past whom I'd feel very uncomfortable having to call up and check my facts with. And I never kept notes or a journal because, frankly, I didn't think anyone would ever give a damn.

By the time Diana and I got together for our lunch, I had already settled on my hero's ethnicity but little else. Over salad I mentioned in passing the book I was planning to write, and the Slovenian element interested Diana because she was of Serbian descent; her maiden name, she told me, was Yakovich. As we ate and got to know each other, we spoke, as strangers often do, of our families. I told her about my children, Valerie and Darren, and she told me about her brothers, Bob and Milan . . .

It hit me at once. *Milan Yakovich*—the strongest, most honest ethnic name I'd ever heard. I asked Diana if her brother would mind if I named my detective after him. She said she didn't think so, but hastened to assure me that in real life he was not a detective at all, but a dentist in Parma.

I am happy to report that, thirteen books later, he is the most famous dentist in Parma.

Only a small part of that is due to me. The real Milan Yakovich was an all-state wrestling champion at Kent State

University—a fact I didn't know when I made my fictional Milan a Kent State alumnus. I used Kent instead of another local school because during my first stay in Cleveland, an old high school and college chum whom I hadn't seen for about thirty years—Michael Schwartz—saw an interview I did on a local news show and contacted me. At the time, Michael was president of Kent State (he's the only one of my high school pals who has a building named after him and a full-length oil portrait of himself) and he treated me to a campus tour, so that by the time I began writing the novel I knew a tiny bit more about that school than any of the other local ones. (Michael then moved on to become the president of Cleveland State University.) Dr. Milan Yakovich is also a civic leader and one of the most respected men in the southern suburbs—his notoriety as the namesake of a fictional gumshoe is only icing on the cake.

I later changed the spelling of Milan's last name. Jacovich, I was told, was a more traditional Slovenian or Croatian spelling than Yakovich.

Several years later Milan and Diana's elderly aunt got me on the phone one day and said, "Why you call my nephew Slovenian? He *Serb!*"

Both the real and the fictional Milans pronounce their name the same way. Over the years I have given many speeches and talks around Ohio, and whenever I am introduced I always cringe a little, because even though I spell out the pronunciation phonetically in every single book—MY-lan YOCK-o-vitch—I am amazed at the different ways most people find to say it. Even my longtime agent insists on calling him "MEE-lahn," and others call him "Mi-LAHN," like the city in Italy, instead of the American pronunciation, MY-lan. Of course, the last name gets mangled even more.

Whenever I do a radio interview for a new book, especially

on the morning *Lanigan and Malone Show* on WMJI-FM, Dr. Yakovich always gets a raft of concerned phone calls at his office from patients who didn't listen to the radio all that carefully and are convinced that their dentist is somehow involved with a murder. He's always remarkably good-natured about it.

Like any author, I have a vivid picture of all my characters in my head, but it wasn't until I'd come back to Cleveland from Los Angeles for perhaps the fourth time that Diana Montagino showed up at a book signing at Booksellers on Chagrin Boulevard—now dearly missed—with a good-looking young man in tow. I had to do a triple take. After writing three books using his name, I'd never before met the real-life Milan, and I was stunned to find out that except for height—my fictional character is six foot three and the real Milan is about five foot ten—that was exactly the face I'd been envisioning each time I sat down to write. The strong Slavic planes of his cheeks and jaw and the merry eyes fit my fictional conceit of private eye Milan perfectly.

A smidgen of irony: when I finally decided to move here and buy a house in Cleveland Heights, Shaker Heights, or University Heights, a Cleveland acquaintance called me in Los Angeles and told me that in case I couldn't find a house right away she knew a woman who was leaving the area for a year to go to Europe and wanted to sublet her apartment—on Cedar Road and Fairmount, just across the street from The Mad Greek restaurant. The offer sounded really bizarre because in my first book, already written and published, I had set my private investigator's apartment in precisely the same place, on Cedar and Fairmount across from The Mad Greek!

I wound up buying a home sometime in October of 1990 and moved there in December, but have often thought about that apartment I never wound up renting as an omen of things to come. I never dreamed my fortunes would become so inextricably enmeshed with that of Milan Jacovich, private eye.

I've become good friends with Dr. Milan Yakovich and his family over the past fifteen years, despite the fact that I've dragged the poor man's name through a lot of sleazy fictional adventures. He's never complained. Once he even asked me to use the name of an old high school friend of his as a minor character. I demurred; if I made a habit out of that, I'd be going crazy with requests. Then I heard the old friend's name: Nello Trinetti.

For a guy like me who writes extensively about the Italian Cosa Nostra in most of my novels, the name Nello Trinetti was made in heaven. The fictional Nello appears as a slick-talking out-of-town hit man in *The Cleveland Connection*, and the real Nello, one of Dr. Milan's oldest and best pals, was thrilled to death when I wrote that the character was extremely good-looking and a "babe magnet."

I've thanked Milan Yakovich publicly on the acknowledgment page of many of my novels, but it won't hurt to do so again. In mystery-writing circles, his name—hard for so many to pronounce—has become synonymous with "the Cleveland guy."

So have I, in a way. I can't go anywhere in America without being asked about the city, its sports teams, its weather, and its culture. If I've become a de facto spokesperson for the place I live, I'm proud to tell people what I like about it. I don't mind telling you what I don't like about the town, either—but just like your own head-shaking stories about your Uncle George who spits when he talks, or your grandmother who makes a point of asking young women their preferred method of birth control, I tell the bad things with love and affection.

I tell them with hope, too. This is a city and a region full of fine, hardworking people from diverse ethnic backgrounds

who deserve better than they've been getting from the powerful special-interest groups who make it their business to en-
sure no progress takes place anywhere they don't have a piece
of the pie.

That hope paid off for me in many ways, because my fifteen
years here have turned me into a pretty good guy, when all
is said and done. Both Milans—the fictional one who solves
murders and spells his name with a *J* and the real one who
works on your teeth and spells his name with a *Y*—are good
guys, too.

Cleveland guys.

CHAPTER 3

A Little Old Man in Jersey

MAKING BETWEEN TEN and twenty speeches every year at libraries and clubs and to school groups, I'm always asked questions about my writing, and one comes up fairly often: "Where do you get your ideas?" Someone always wants to know. Sometimes when I'm feeling particularly flippant I'll swear that whenever I need some, I contact an old guy in New Jersey who sends me ten ideas for twenty-five bucks.

Once, when I was teaching an adult writing class at a college just outside Los Angeles, a woman from the group called me one afternoon.

"I have six different ideas for books," she told me on the phone. "But I can't think of which one to pick."

Since she didn't explain any of those ideas further, everything in me wanted to simply say, "Pick number four" and hang up. Instead, I said, "All of us have dozens of different ideas every day. As a writer, pick the one you're thinking about the most."

She thanked me profusely—and we never spoke about it again. But I've always felt that way—that certain ideas go in one ear and out the other while others, the really important ones, stay inside the head and cook and boil until they simply have to be written.

I recall an important and disturbing idea that eventually evolved into a Milan Jacovich book, *The Dutch*.

It was back in the early seventies, in Los Angeles, when I heard from a coworker on a TV show about the suicide of an acquaintance of both of ours. "She did the Dutch," he told me. I was confused and asked him for more specifics and he stretched it out. "The Dutch Act," he explained. "She committed suicide."

That was more than a decade before I started writing detective novels, but I asked around in Hollywood and heard from several people about "the Dutch." Not many people knew where that slang originated, but I knew when I sat down and wrote the Milan Jacovich adventure about a distraught father asking the private eye to investigate why his daughter had taken her own life.

Right from the start I decided quite easily how the character would die. The Lorain-Carnegie Bridge stretching across the Cuyahoga River—also now called "The William Hope Memorial Bridge" after the stonemason father of the late comedian/icon Bob Hope—was and is extremely beautiful because there are gigantic statues of the "Titans of Industry" wrapped around each of the bridge's pylons. It was easy to figure out why the fictional victim had fallen from the bridge and onto the hard ground nearly two hundred feet below instead of into the water, and the more I researched the more excited I grew about putting this novel together.

I typed the first sentence of that novel: "The dark space under the Lorain-Carnegie Bridge is, I think, a singularly lousy place to die." That one sentence really ignited my imagination, and I never let up.

•   •   •

MY EX-WIFE, GAIL, whose marriage to me ended in 1978 but with whom I remained good friends until her untimely death early in 2005, was living in her hometown of Denver in the early nineties, and her oldest friend from high school was running for a seat on the Denver City Council. Gail called to tell me about the campaign and said, "You really have to come out here and see it for yourself—you'll just never believe it. I think there's a book in this campaign for sure."

So I spent a week in Denver, going to political rallies and planning sessions, and was amused and startled by the ineptness of Gail's childhood friend's campaign, especially against a popular and well-entrenched incumbent. The tumblers in my mind began clicking away at the very first rally; I knew where I was going with this idea—or rather where Milan would. I came back to Cleveland, transferred the rather peculiar politics I'd witnessed in Colorado to a mayoral race in a nonexistent northeastern suburb (I called it Lake Erie Shores, so I wouldn't upset the real-life politicians in Lake County who, I'm certain, would have taken offense and believed I was talking about *them*) and wrote *The Lake Effect*. I interviewed several Cleveland-area people involved in local politics, and while some readers might find the chicanery, maneuvering, and stupid political mistakes in the novel unrealistic, I assure you that everything I wrote really happened somewhere, sometime—except the murder, of course.

Although I wrote about politics in *The Lake Effect*, I was careful not to insert my own political beliefs into the mix. Those who know me well are more than aware of how I vote in local and national elections, because I'm pretty vocal about it. As a matter of fact, I've only missed one or two elections in more than forty years. But I don't think it's fair to sneak my political agenda into a mystery novel, anymore than it's fair to proselytize about religion, either. If anyone is remotely interested in my political or religious beliefs, buy me a drink sometime and we can talk about it—maybe, if I just happen to be in the mood. But you won't find it in my novels. I figure most people are like me—if we want to be preached to or harangued, there's a church or synagogue on almost every Cleveland corner, and it will only cost you a buck dropped into the collection plate, too. My books are written mostly for entertainment.

In direct contrast to *The Lake Effect,* the germ of *The Cleveland Local* was not politics but an actual murder. The story came from a friend who had been on a vacation in the Caribbean when a young Canadian man in her tour group was shot-gunned to death early one morning while jogging on a lonely beach. The local police were not very keen on investigation and wound up sweeping the murder under the rug. Noreen Koppelman Goldstein told the true story and supplied me with a few newspaper articles on the subject, and then I went to work. This one was difficult from its inception: how does a murder on a remote Caribbean island involve a private investigator from Cleveland, Ohio, one Milan Jacovich, who never met the victim in his life and has never been on a vacation to that part of the world? I'm pleased to report that I figured it out. (The title, *The Cleveland Local,* made some readers think before reading it that it was about a train. It's not—"local" refers to a made-up union in Cleveland. Similarly, a few years later, when I wrote another Milan adventure story, *The Indian Sign,* I had to assure almost everyone that the novel was not about baseball.)

Once in a great while, a friend—someone without an agenda who doesn't want to see their name next to mine on the book jacket—will speedball an idea past me that really catches on, and I wind up writing the novel—all by myself. I've already mentioned my late ex-wife Gail's involvement in suggesting the back story for *The Lake Effect.* Even my granddaughter, Shea Holland Thompson, got into the act by ruminating on an idea that I chewed on for a while before deciding how I could make it work in what I hope will be an upcoming novel. And my pal Josh Pachter, a well-known author of mystery short stories and an excellent teacher, and his daughter, Becca Jones, literally handed me an idea. I turned it down at first, saying that I'm not the guy to write this story, and even suggested Josh write it himself. But I thought about it for a few weeks and realized what an amazing story it is. So I called Josh back to announce that it's knocking on the inside of my chest trying to get out, and I'm chafing at the bit to write it now. I'll start it as soon as I finish this memoir.

My friend Jane Bauschard was responsible for the creation of two of my books. She invited me to visit the ceramics studio of her brother, James O'Brien, just off Superior Avenue in the mid-thirties, in an amazing old studio building, which led me on a trail of conjecture that eventually became *The Duke of Cleveland*. I described the building almost brick for brick, including the old freight elevator that used to haul newly manufactured barbed wire at the beginning of the twentieth century, and even the body of a dead pigeon up on the roof. And one night, during intermission at the Cleveland Play House, Jane told me of a news story she'd read somewhere that, after many twists and turns, became *Collision Bend*. I dedicated that one to her.

Now, every time I see Collision Bend from the window of The Avenue at Tower City or from some other office overlooking the city, I feel a connection with that special river curve, especially when I think about the relatively gruesome ending of the novel. Similarly, I think of Milan's adventures in *The Irish Sports Pages* whenever I walk into an Irish pub like Nighttown.

I had heard somewhere that the newspaper obituary section was called the "Irish sports pages" because in the old days the Irish politicians who used to gather at Tony's Restaurant on West 117th Street for breakfast every morning, unlike most guys who check the sports pages for the previous day's scores, used to turn to the death notices first to see who in their constituency had died, and would plan the rest of their day's activities around attending the wake.

Oddly enough, I couldn't find anyone who'd ever heard the expression before, so I called the now-retired longtime ethnic affairs reporter for the *Plain Dealer*, William F. Miller. He'd never heard of the Irish sports pages, either, but being a veteran newshound, he spent the afternoon phoning a few sources and called me several hours later with a confirmation: some of the older Irish politicians still remembered the death notices and the wakes they read about every single morning in the *Plain Dealer* or the now defunct *Cleveland Press*. I have no idea in which Irish bar Bill Miller actually found the answer that afternoon. (Bill, by the way, is a hell of a guy and, at Irish and Slovenian parties, a lovely tenor singer as well.)

That book was inspired by a news story in which a real-life Ohio public figure was royally scammed by a con man claiming to be just off the plane from the Ould Sod. I simply took the news report, slightly changed the names to fictional ones so no real people would get in trouble, stirred in a murder, and gave it to Milan Jacovich to take care of.

The Cleveland Connection was jump-started by a visit to Milwaukee, where I ate a magnificent dinner in a Serbian restaurant and had a long talk with the owner, who was a student of history, born in Serbia in the late 1940s. He happened to mention the slaughter of the Serbs by the Nazis during World War II, almost as horrible a massacre as occurred elsewhere in Europe against the Jews. How did that translate into a modern-day Milan Jacovich novel fifty years later? I guess you'll have to read the book. (People tell me that of all the Milan adventures I've written, this particular one is the most "ethnic" of them all.)

There is one fairly recent real-life Cleveland event that's been gnawing at me for quite a while now, but I can't seem to make it fit as fiction: a canvas sack containing about four hundred thousand dollars actually fell off the back of an armored truck downtown several years ago, and was picked up by a passerby, who returned it the next day after listening to dire threats from the FBI and the rest of the federal government. I've started two different books featuring an unexpected windfall like that, but I always seem to bog down in the middle. So if anyone has an idea how to make it work on the page—just let me know.

A few years back, I quietly celebrated, as I always do, finishing a novel and sending it off to New York. It was summertime, and even though a new book inside me was just waiting to be written, I decided I'd take about two weeks off and have myself a little break. So I went to the Cleveland Heights Public Library, which is only a few blocks from my house, and collected so many books I wanted to read that when I stacked them one atop the other the shaky construction reached nearly to my waist. I went home, poured myself a giant glass of iced tea, took a book from the top of the pile out onto my deck, and began what was supposed to be two weeks' worth of reading.

About twenty minutes into the first book—and I frankly don't remember the title—I got an idea to add to my next novel, and decided I'd go inside to my computer and just jot the note down so I wouldn't forget it.

Two hours later, I'd already written the first three pages of the new book, and the stack of reading material I'd so carefully selected from the library shelves was destined to be ignored. Writing is like that. Even though I'll never pull in the kind of money Stephen King does every year, I constantly find myself driven to continue—to create.

CHAPTER 4

Watch Out!

MANY PEOPLE LIKE the idea of having their names appear in my works. They want a ticket into Milan's fictional world, and are even willing to pay for it in the form of a charity event that auctions off "character" names. I use real names in almost all my Milan novels now. Most of the folks who want to be immortalized in Milan books don't much care whether the character is good or evil, either; I think some of them actually prefer being portrayed as "bad guys."

After more than a dozen Jacovich novels, I've only had one person complain bitterly about the inclusion of his name in one of my novels. He was and is a local television personality whose real name I merely wrote about in passing before I met him. He wasn't a "character" in the book, just someone well-known I chose to mention to add to the story's Cleveland "color." He hadn't even read the book at the time, yet in our first (and only) meeting, when he found out I'd "used" his name, he threatened to have his attorney contact me. He said he might even sue me, which was and is ridiculous because as a public figure and he had no legal or moral standing to whine about it, whether he liked it or not. He was also clueless enough not to be pleased that I mentioned his name in the book with respect.

The TV personality never did sic his lawyer on me, and I assume he never got around to reading the book, either.

That makes us even, because in all the years since our single conversation, I've never once watched him on television. My guess is neither of us has suffered much because of the altercation, although since then whenever we've been in the same place at the same time we've made a point of not speaking to each other. Life is just too short.

• • •

WHEN I'M INVITED to speak at a library or an organization, the first thing I do is scan the crowd for a face, or faces, that seem somehow interesting to me. It doesn't have to be a beautiful one, but it must be an attention-grabbing face, one with a secret wisdom, a look that will trigger in me an emotional chord that makes me imagine it in various situations that I'll one day use in a novel. After the event, I always jot down a brief description in my notebook or make an entry onto my tape recorder that I might use two, five, or even ten years down the line, long after the subject in question has forgotten they ever met me. It makes sense, after all. If I didn't make notes on people I see, my next novel would be about my drapes, because that's what I look at all day.

Every one of the characters in my books is based on someone I've met or might have noticed on the street or in a restaurant who has what I consider a distinctive look. So if you see me coming, watch out! You may become the inadvertent "star" of one of my books.

Still, I try hard to disguise my subjects. After all, in mysteries almost every character in the book is a suspect and therefore is in some way corrupt. They might not be the murderer, but they certainly have secrets to hide. This was what drove the plot of my second Cleveland novel, *Full Cleveland*, a novel about a group of people with secrets who are stunned when they discover they are all being blackmailed. (Several years later, I actually named one of my Milan novels *The Best-Kept Secret*. Unfortunately, my then-publisher, St. Martin's Press, assigned some in-house flack to write the "flap copy," the teasing material about the book and its contents that appears on the inside front flap of the book cover, and he or she actually gave away the big secret that one of the characters in the novel keeps to himself and that inspired my title.)

So when I meet someone who inspires me, say, a plumber in real life, I'll change their name and make them an attorney, or a mobster, or a college professor. That's why most people don't even recognize themselves, even though their look is something I always keep in my mind as I write them.

Unlike many writers, I happen to be a pretty good speller—for the rest, thank God for computers and spell-checker—and so for several years I was asked to participate in the Plain Dealer Spelling Bee for Literacy, benefiting Project: LEARN, a charity close to my heart because it promotes helping adults learn how to read. I did pretty well as a bee speller, partnered in my first several years with radio personality Rena Blumberg—but we never quite won. We'd come in second, or fourth, always hanging in till nearly the very end, but we couldn't seem to take it all the way. The first two years we were defeated by the same team, two young women who were playing under the corporate sponsorship of American Greetings, where they both worked. They were such good spellers that eventually they retired, giving others a chance. (It was a nice thought, but I never won after they backed out, either.)

Both women were bright, bubbly, and attractive, and one of them, Nicole Hunter, is a tall, cool blonde—the type I was certain Milan Jacovich would fall for. So even though we hardly knew each other, in *The Duke of Cleveland* I introduced the character Nicole Archer. (Archer = hunter. Get it?) I kept Nicole

Archer around as Milan's love interest for several books until, like most women in Milan's life, she got bored with him and moved on. The real Nicole Hunter is in the creative department at American Greetings, but the fictional Nicole Archer is a neonatologist—a doctor specializing in the care of newborn and premature babies. And even *that* came from real life, albeit a different experience altogether—the sister of a woman I used to date in Los Angeles actually *was* a neonatologist.

I wonder if she's read the books.

I suppose a word is in order here about why Milan has been unable to sustain a romance for more than two or three books at a time; it's the question I'm asked most often. "When will Milan get a real, meaningful romantic relationship?"

I used to answer: "When I get one, he'll get one," but that turned out not to be true. I have a major romantic relationship right now, which I'm going to keep close to my heart forever, but it hasn't helped Milan a bit. The real reason is that Milan Jacovich is perceived as being very good at his work but very bad at the rest of his life. His jobs and investigations are first-rate, but personally he's alone and quite lonely—the serious embodiment of Steve Martin's comedic screen personality, "The Lonely Guy." From what readers tell me, especially women, they feel sorry for him and worry about him. If he fell in love and got married, they might stop caring.

I've always felt, too, that a private eye in novels should be free and unencumbered, able to stay all day or all night on a stakeout without having to call home to his wife and say he won't be there for dinner. In the first book, I gave Milan young sons to provide grounding and a sense of real humanity—but they lived with his ex-wife, Lila, and, except for weekends, he had no ongoing responsibility for taking care of them. Sure, it was the easy way out for me—I admit that. But why should a writer beginning a mystery series that would endure for many books yet to come—Milan hung around with me for sixteen years—make it tougher on himself than he has to?

I have to admit I saddled him with some difficult women, especially the ones with whom he carried on a relationship over two and three books at a stretch. They never started out being difficult. But when the relationship with Milan reached a critical stage they were rarely anything *but* difficult. I vividly recall the scene when Milan was "breaking up" with his third long-term lover, Connie Haley, in *The Indian Sign,* and my New York editor scrawled on the manuscript with what seemed to be genuine surprise, "She's a *bitch!*"

There is a character in *The Lake Effect* taken almost directly from real life, and I have to admit it was uncharacteristic for me to include him—but he is the only person in Cleveland in fifteen years who ever went out of his way to be really mean to me. He was a freelance journalist then, for some of the smaller papers, and had decided all by himself to make bashing me in print his hobby. He never criticized my books or my writing, which are fair game, but said some unbelievably nasty things about me personally whenever he could—even when writing a column about something else unrelated and strangely squeezing in my name. Perhaps he was jealous of me because he wrote for small newspapers while I was on the local bestseller list and was paid for making speeches all over the area, or angry with me because at the time I was dating the woman who had gone out with him and then dropped him a full two years before I ever came to town. For whatever reason it was obvious he had it in for me.

The character I created from him was also a journalist, and I described him as looking and acting exactly the way his real-life counterpart did, even giving him the same initials. And in the novel I made him out to be as much of an ineffectual horse's ass as he was in real life. I've never done a character quite so on-the-nose as this in a book before or since, but I'm pleased to say that after *The Lake Effect* made its debut, the man never wrote another word about me. As a matter of fact, he left town shortly thereafter. I wish I could take credit for that, but the truth probably lies in another direction.

Moral: Never mess with somebody who has a public forum, like a book series—especially if he learned how to be rough and tough after twenty-four years in the snake pit known as Hollywood. I don't consider myself a bad guy at all, but one should think twice before stepping on my blue suede shoes.

•   •   •

VIVIAN TRUSCOTT, A character I've used in several books, is the tall, blonde, beautiful, regal-looking Cleveland TV news anchorwoman at Channel 12—and Cleveland doesn't really *have* a Channel 12—who first appears in *Full Cleveland* and later plays a major role in *Collision Bend*. In the books—and *only in the books,* not in real life—before she was a tall, blonde, regal-looking news anchor in Cleveland, Vivian Truscott was a tall, blonde, beautiful call girl in Las Vegas.

I wrote *Full Cleveland* in Los Angeles in about 1988, and at the time I had no idea I would one day be living here, so I didn't particularly worry whether individual Clevelanders would recognize themselves in my books—or care. So Vivian was fashioned, in appearance only, by my memories of Wilma Smith, then at Channel 5 and currently with Fox 8 News, whose newscasts I had watched during my first trip here.

Normally I never "tell" who inspired my characters. It's one of the few secrets we writers have left, since writing fiction is like getting naked in public; we are constantly exposing ourselves, whether we mean to or not—and if we didn't in some way use people we know to populate our novels, we'd soon be writing about Martians. So whenever I was asked publicly or privately about Vivian, I always kept my own counsel—until some time in 1991, just after I'd come here to stay, when I found myself at a party and there, across the room, looking at me and heading my way, was Wilma Smith.

We had never met before, and so I was bracing myself, figuring I was going to wear home the contents of the glass she had in her hand. But Wilma is as warm, friendly, and genuine in person as she is on television, and after we introduced ourselves she told me how much she enjoyed reading my work and how pleased she was I had decided to make Cleveland my real home. After about five minutes, though, she looked furtively around as if she were about to ask a very embarrassing question, leaned toward me, and whispered, "Was that *me?*"

Nailed! I felt like Jack Nicholson at the end of the film *Terms of Endearment*—I was ten seconds away from a clean getaway! There didn't seem any way around it, though, so I sputtered and coughed and stammered, saying that all my characters were a composite of a lot of different people, and finally telling her Vivian Truscott was based mostly on a local anchorwoman from Los Angeles.

Wilma's face fell in disappointment. "I wanted it to be me," she said. That really surprised me, given the nature of Vivian Truscott's previous occupation. But I finally admitted she had been my "model" for the character, and we laughed about it and became friends.

Some years later, while researching *Collision Bend*, which is a novel about the killing of a local TV personality, I asked her to lunch so I could pick her brain. My Hollywood years had taught me much about entertainment television but virtually nothing about the news operation, and I really needed someone who had been front and center in a local newsroom to tell me how it worked. Her input was more helpful than I ever dreamed; I couldn't have written that book nearly so well without her help.

However, when we walked into the restaurant together—it was Hornblower's on the lake right next to Burke Lakefront Airport—everybody immediately noticed her. Even if you didn't know who she is, Wilma Smith is a tall, breathtaking beauty who is going to attract attention everywhere she goes. But on that afternoon as we made our way toward the back of the restaurant, she leaned over to me *in all seriousness* and said, "See how famous you are in Cleveland? Everybody's looking at you."

• • •

OTHER THAN ONE journalist mentioned above, the press has been extremely kind to me ever since I came to town, including WMJI Radio's John Lanigan and Jimmy Malone, who never say no when I want to plug my books on their top-rated morning drive-time show and whose names I've mentioned in almost every Milan Jacovich adventure. Come to think of it, maybe that's why they keep inviting me onto their show. They have, at times, called me up at eight o'clock in the morning to talk on the program when I had no reason to be visiting at all, and I had to slap my cheeks awake while I did so.

When Tony Rizzo, now the Channel 8 sports coanchor, was a regular on the *Lanigan and Malone Show*, I had him inadvertently supply the major clue that helped Milan solve one of his cases, in *Collision Bend*. The *Lanigan and Malone Show* is crazy fun for the most part, anarchy and laughter and interaction with call-in listeners, but John Lanigan also happens to be one of the best interviewers of politicians I've ever heard, and it's a pleasure for me listening to him hold their feet to the fire whenever they appear as guests on the show. He and

Malone also have a great time laughing with their guest comedians, often in town for a stretch at Hilarities.

In *A Shoot in Cleveland*, the site of the murder was a house on the lake in Bay Village, a community in which John Lanigan happens to live. When I did the show to talk about the book, he braced me on it in his usually funny and aggressive way, saying he resented my using his hometown for a murder.

I said, "John, as my grandmother used to tell me, everything is not about *you*!" It was the only time I ever startled him into momentary silence, but Jimmy Malone and his on-air staff jokers, Chip Kullik and sports maven Mark "Munch" Bishop, all actually rose to their feet to give me a standing ovation for that one.

I've also appeared on the radio several times with the velvet-voiced Dee Perry of WCPN, and on shows on WGAR, WTAM, and a solid number of other stations over the years that I've forgotten. Thank you all.

The *Plain Dealer* became my favorite newspaper from the moment I settled down here, and they always give me lovely publicity. Columnist Sarah Crump and her late predecessor, Mary Strassmeyer, were always there to talk with and about me, and "The Minister of Culture," Michael Heaton—whose father was an iconic sports columnist for many years before I moved to Cleveland and whose sister, Patricia Heaton, spent nine years costarring as the Emmy-winning TV wife of Ray Romano on the sitcom *Everybody Loves Raymond*—did several wonderful pieces about me, and all my Milan Jacovich books got reviewed in the Books section on Sunday. The reviews were not always positive, either.

Also at the *Plain Dealer* are the book editors who've put up with my monthly book review columns for the last eighteen years, which I began writing in 1989, even before I moved here from Los Angeles. Janice Harayda, Karen Sandstrom, and

Karen Long each edit in a slightly different and creative way, and I've enjoyed working for all of them. I've done monthly columns for the past thirteen years or so for *Currents*, the life-style section of the *Chagrin Valley Times,* working first with a dear friend and newspaper editor, Martha Towns—who was the very first journalist in Cleveland to conduct a one-on-one interview with me when I was just visiting in 1988—and most recently with Kelli McClellan. Articles I've written have also appeared in *Cleveland Magazine* and *Northern Ohio Live.*

Several reporters from nearby counties have been wonderful to me, too, including Sandra Fahning and Russ Massara. Without the support of the media, some of the best talent in the world would sink into oblivion, so I'm very grateful for all the nice things said about me by my press pals here.

There is one fictional journalist we should talk about, who has made an appearance in every one of the Milan Jacovich books. His name is Ed Stahl. He's one of Milan's best friends, and he's always there to give Milan a helping hand because he knows everything worth knowing in the city of Cleveland. He also has a Pulitzer Prize in the bottom drawer of his desk, something the real *Plain Dealer* had gone without for some fifty-six years until the richly deserved award went in 2005 to the brilliant columns of Connie Schultz.

Many have asked me whether Ed Stahl was created in the image of Dick Feagler, a gifted and trenchant columnist I *never* miss reading, even when I sometimes disagree with him. Feagler was for a time the Channel 3 news anchorman, and for the past several years has had his own TV show on the PBS station, WVIZ, where he interviews other columnists, politicians, and once in a while *me*. Okay, let's examine the differences between the two of them: Ed Stahl comes from a German immigrant family, and wears glasses that make him look like Clark Kent on a bad day; he is cranky, cantankerous, contentious, in-your-face, knows everything that goes on in his city, and he's positively unafraid of stepping on anyone's toes no matter how important. Ed Stahl, during his fictional life, is slightly overweight, he enjoys his whiskey a little too much, and constantly smokes a malodorous pipe. He even puffs away at his desk in the otherwise smoke-free environs of the *Plain Dealer,* and everyone there is far too intimidated by him to make him stop.

Well, that proves the real man and the fictional one are not the same at all, because everyone knows Dick Feagler doesn't smoke a pipe.

· · ·

I USE MANY people I've met even briefly as characters, changing the names most of the time. I have one hard-and-fast rule, though, about using real people as models for my created fictional people: I never cannibalize the persona of anyone I really love. It would be too difficult for me to separate the real person from the fictional one. I've used the first names of both my children, Valerie and Darren, mainly because they asked me to, but in both cases I had a different physical vision of the character—the artist named "Valerie" in *The Duke of Cleveland* was older than my daughter, and I envisioned her as lanky and red-haired whereas my daughter is dark with big Hershey Kiss eyes. The egotistical actor "Darren" in *A Shoot in Cleveland* was, in my mind's eye, a specific movie star (I knew who he was but didn't name him) who is a little bit of a jerk, and is as different from my own son as it's humanly possible to be. He is, as I acknowledged in the foreword of the novel, possessed of "killer good looks" like my son, but he looks nothing like Darren Roberts.

My granddaughter, Shea Thompson, has just turned fourteen, now getting to the age when it's okay for her to read my books, and she's asked me to create a fictional Shea, too. Unfortunately I can't write about a fourteen-year-old Shea from Aspen with periwinkle blue eyes and a sunny smile and kindness, compassion, talent, intelligence and wit; that would be too close to the truth. Maybe I'll make my make-believe Shea an elderly lady who feeds stray cats, grows roses, and solves murders.

But who ever heard of an elderly lady named Shea?

CHAPTER 5

All Around Town

FRIENDS AND ACQUAINTANCES are always hammering me with real "settings" for my mysteries. "Wouldn't it be great if they discovered a body in the Great Hall of the Library?" one will say. Or, "How about *Murder at the Cleveland Orchestra?* You could set the whole book at Severance Hall."

They are all colorful suggestions, but the good folk who run those places would not be pleased if I wrote about their venues in a murderous fashion. That's why in my books, most "bodies" are found in their own homes, or in neutral places like a riverbank or a deserted street. I've never written a novel in which a Cleveland sport was integral to the plot, and I probably never will. I'm certain that even if a fictional Browns or Tribe superstar were to wind up murdered in my pages, I'd be in more trouble with Cleveland than I ever dreamed.

Author Margaret Truman, who spent much of her youth in the nation's capital when her father, Harry, was a senator, then vice president, and finally president of the United States, has been successful in staging her fictional murders in public places in Washington (*Murder on Capitol Hill*, etc.) because what awful things can you say about Washington institutions that haven't been said already?

My first three books about Cleveland and private investigator Milan Jacovich were written while I was still living in Los Angeles. Despite my frequent trips back to do research or to promote the earlier books, I'm sure I got a lot of things about the city all wrong because I wasn't able to jump into the car and drive somewhere close by to solidify my impressions the way I've been doing since moving here in the closing days of 1990.

But I had great Cleveland memories from my first trip back in 1987, thanks to some of the good friends I made here. It didn't take me long to become enamored of the fantastic restaurants and nightclubs, the Play House, the Cleveland Museum of Art and the Cleveland Orchestra, the then-thriving Cleveland Ballet, Amish country and the nearby city of Akron whose growth I've been so pleased to watch for the past fifteen years, and the general "feel" of Northeast Ohio. I tried to load as many of those memories as I could into the first few books.

Johnny's Bar on Fulton Avenue, for instance, is a place where I've set many scenes, because my first real trip there was such a memorable one. Rick and Betsy Alexander had raved about it and invited me to meet them for dinner one cold winter's evening. Their directions didn't prepare me for how Johnny's Bar looked from the outside—a corner bar in a blue-collar neighborhood with a neon sign that looked as though it dated from the Art Deco 1930s.

It still looks that way, possibly the most deceptive-looking entryway to any fine restaurant in America. And when I went inside for the first time—this was long before they remodeled the place into the small, elegant restaurant it's now become—the front room looked like a working-class tavern. Several of the men at the bar were in overalls or red and black plaid shirts—and they were puffing away at Camels and encircling their shot and a beer with a protective arm. The waiter, with an interestingly bent nose and a manner of reciting from memory the specials of the day that channels Joe Pesci in a film like *Goodfellas*, looked like a recently retired welterweight. I still couldn't shake the feeling that Rick and Betsy were perpetuating a huge joke on an unsuspecting visitor from Southern California.

That lasted until the food arrived, and it was spectacular—one of the best places I've ever eaten anywhere in the country. Johnny's Bar is one of the great restaurants in any city; I patronized it several more times before I had to go back to Los Angeles, and when I finally moved here three years later it was one of the first places I headed. Johnny's has since opened two more restaurants downtown, and I've visited both of them often, but for me there will always be something special about Johnny's Bar across the street from Saint Rocco's Church. It's intimate, it's classy, and there's just something about it that says "Cleveland." Upscale, and yet blue-collar—it's that combo that makes it so charming.

Cleveland, like all other cities, changes rapidly, and not always for the better, and 1987 was a long time ago. Some of the places I frequented back in the good old days are now gone: the Watermark, Tangerine Fahrley's and D'Poo's on the River, and Sammy's, which exists today in the Flats and the east side as banquet centers but not as an everyday restaurant. They were all on the east bank, and I still miss the incredible views of the river traffic going by so close to Sammy's window it seemed as if you could reach out and touch it. The Flats was the leading tourist attraction in Ohio for a while and then, almost overnight, it fell upon hard times. Now most of the fun nightspots and eateries are closed and you can almost see the tumbleweeds bouncing through the deserted streets.

Another place many of us working on the *Cash Explosion* show used to go for lunch was called Mo's East Side, located on Chagrin Boulevard just west of Pepper Pike. As I recall, it wasn't a terrific restaurant, but the lunches it served were honest and decent, and it was close to our office; the small program staff enjoyed our gatherings there. It's long-gone now, replaced by a lovely Spanish restaurant, Marbella—but I can still taste the memories.

The Silver Grille was one of the most elegant restaurants in town, also long gone even though books have been written about it. Typical, too, is the Theatrical Grill on Short Vincent Street downtown, which welcomed professional athletes, show business celebrities, movers and shakers from the legal and business districts, and both cops and mobsters, from here and all over. About a year after I called it the Jesters and included it in one of my novels, the restaurant closed its doors—but virtually no one in Cleveland who read my book was fooled into believing it was anyplace besides the Theatrical.

Many of the other restaurants on which I cut my Cleveland teeth are still around. At least twice a week we'd enjoy an excellent bar lunch and a beer at the Winking Lizard Tavern on Miles Road; when I used the setting in *Deep Shaker*, I thinly disguised it by calling it the Blind Frog Saloon because to my knowledge there are no drug pushers hanging out at the Winking Lizard, and they certainly would not have countenanced the fistfight I staged with Milan in their parking lot. They later expanded and now have several Lizards all around the Greater Cleveland and Akron area.

I lunched often at Corky and Lenny's in Cedar Center until it closed up and concentrated all its efforts on its sister restaurant on Chagrin Boulevard. I also ate frequently at Jack's Deli, on Green and Cedar across the street from Heinen's Market, and during the lunch hour I almost always had to wait in line. I have sent Milan in there for breakfast or lunch on several occasions to enjoy what I consider the east side's best corned beef sandwich—frankly even better than the famous Slyman's deli just east of downtown—or their potato *latkes* or their matzo brie. Jack's Deli is still here, busier than ever. It's moved a few doors down, still in the same shopping area but in a larger space—and I still go there a lot for lunch when I'm not watching my weight and my cholesterol. I miss the wallpaper in the big back dining room in the old location, though—wonderful caricatures by the late cartoonist Al Hirschfeld of Broadway and film stars. I'll bet you couldn't have named all of the celebrities.

During that initial stay in 1987 I can't count how many dinners I enjoyed at Nighttown, at the top of Cedar Hill in Cleveland Heights. I remember one blizzardy Sunday night when I met Jim and Eileen Terry-Reed and their friend Lynda Silverberg (who would later become my realtor and find the house in which I'm now typing these words), and we sat in Nighttown for hours and hours, eating and drinking and laughing so hard and so loudly that I was certain we were going to be unceremoniously tossed out into the deep snow. After I moved here permanently, Nighttown became a favorite for me because Milan, who lives less than two blocks away, goes there a lot, too.

I also hung out at Noggins, in the Van Aken shopping plaza in Shaker Heights—one of those bars in which no one is a stranger. One of my closest friends, David Welsh, who moved to Shaker from Mansfield about ninety miles south, eventually became a part of Noggins' family. When he and his new love, Julia, got married early in 2005, the big reception after the ceremony was, of all places, at Noggins.

During my first visit, the Lion and the Lamb, in Pepper Pike, was a late-night refuge for me. Joey Sands was the maestro of the piano bar back then, and he's there eighteen years later, playing the great tunes on the grand piano from the classic American songbook by Cole Porter and Rodgers and Hart and Jerome Kern that we rarely get to hear anywhere else. That's my kind of popular music. This is one of the few bars in the area where I can listen to it, and when I've had enough to drink, even sing—but I don't do that much anymore. In my first Cleveland novel, *Pepper Pike*, Milan Jacovich visits the Lion and the Lamb in the first chapter, although I don't name it, and I even cheat a little by writing that it's located on Chagrin Boulevard. (Well, it *almost* is!) Two years later, when I was visiting here and dropped into the L & L again, everyone in there had read my book and recognized me from the old days. It's a warm and cozy joint. (Milan returned there in *The Indian Sign*.)

I still patronize all those eating and drinking establishments. In the ensuing years, Cleveland has become a much more sophisticated restaurant town, and I like some of the newer places as well—some of which have also come and gone, like the Greek Isles and Circo and Kosta's—but the older joints exert a nostalgic pull on me, because it was within their confines I learned to love my adopted city.

•   •   •

IN MY EARLIEST Jacovich books I changed the names of most of the restaurants and bars, although anyone who knows Cleveland can pick them out easily. The Watermark, for instance, in *Pepper Pike* became The Watershed. Sammy's turned into Danny's. In the fourth book in the series, *The Cleveland Connection*, the famed old Theatrical Grill, which throughout history was a sizzling restaurant, a jazz venue, and a swinging nightclub joint on Short Vincent Street, was called in my book The Jesters and was characterized as a good-natured haven for gangsters like the fictional Nello Trinetti, and for hookers and crooked politicians. Sadly, the Theatrical Grill closed several years later.

I've often been asked why I instituted the name changes, and I have a couple of reasons.

When I was still living in Los Angeles and writing about Cleveland, I wasn't sure whether the restaurateurs here would be happy having their places appear in a mystery novel. Mysteries, after all, smack of murder and corruption and all sorts of dark doings, and I didn't want to offend anyone, especially restaurant owners I'd never even met. More importantly, if I was going to say that a certain establishment was a "mob" hangout, or that something even the slightest bit untoward happened there, I felt safer using a made-up name. Nobody wants the image of a dead body in their restaurant, even if it's just in a novel. It was only after I moved here that I realized most restaurants were anxious to have their names mentioned in my books, so I began using real places, although I did create one restaurant from my imagination, in *A Shoot in Cleveland*, and stuck with it for several books thereafter. I called it the White Magnolia, locating it vaguely in one of the west suburbs, Rocky River. Milan Jacovich had a three-book romance with a pigtailed blonde named Connie Haley, the daughter of the White Magnolia's owner. Just after *A Shoot* was published, a very close friend of mine, a lovely lady in her eighties, called me to complain that she had tried to take friends to the White Magnolia for dinner the previous weekend but couldn't find the establishment in the phone book or by calling information. I said it was fictional, that it didn't exist. She said, "Why would you do that? You write about Johnny's Bar all the time, and that exists."

I explained to her that I never said Milan Jacovich was sleeping with Johnny's daughter, either. There is more than one reason for an author to disguise the name of an establishment.

Back in 1992 when my daughter, son-in-law, and then-toddling granddaughter were visiting Cleveland, I took them on a riverboat cruise of the Cuyahoga, where I heard the guide describe the area of the river just across from Tower City (Jacobs Field wasn't built yet) where the current takes an abrupt 180-degree turn as Collision Bend, because in the old days it was common for some of the six-hundred-foot ore boats that ply the waters to have aquatic fender benders trying to negotiate that hairpin curve. I thought it was a terrific name for a sharp bend in the river and an even better title for a novel about Cleveland.

And in case you've always wondered, Collision Bend is *not* another title for Dead Man's Curve on the Inner Belt. One colorful name per location is enough. But it's startling how many longtime Clevelanders never heard the expression.

Shortly thereafter I drove down to Collision Bend, where the Eagle Avenue Bridge is, and made a notebook full of observations about it. Then, since it was a raw early spring day and I was a bit chilly, I dropped into the legendary Jim's Steak House right on the point for a beer. That's when I met a man who has become one of my best Cleveland buddies, public relations maven Ron Watt. We spent a long afternoon there—back then I could match him drink for drink—and became close friends. After that we got together many times at Jim's Steak House for lunch despite the certain knowledge that their steak sandwich and home fries was a heart attack on a plate. It's still the best I've had anywhere. The bar's atmosphere drew laborers, cops, newspaper reporters, idle millionaires, married cheaters, and some of the top names in Cleveland's corporate world—all who loved their toddies—to a cocktail lounge that only had six stools.

Jim's had a magnificent river view from its main dining room, but we always hung out in the dark, enclosed back bar for the entire afternoon, only occasionally glancing up at the muted TV set, and enjoyed the mixology and friendship of the affable bartender, the late Ray Macaskee. I was so taken with Jim's that when I began *Collision Bend* I had Milan Jacovich move his office down there, to a building right next door to the restaurant so he could go in for lunch all the time.

To all the readers who have asked me about Milan's office building, I admit it doesn't exist. There is a warehouse next to the restaurant right now, but it's hardly a fit place for anyone to have an office. And it doesn't fit the description I give it in the books.

Sadly for the novels and for a whole trainload of its former habitués, Jim's Steak House closed a few years later, and now Milan has to eat lunch somewhere else. So do I. While Ron and I have found other great places for lunch—Johnny's Bar on Fulton, Johnny's Downtown, Swingos on the Lake, and my particular favorite, the venerable Ferris Steak House on Detroit Road—the ambiance is never quite the same. Ron Watt is on a first-name basis with the bartenders in all of them, which inspired me to have Milan Jacovich ruminate on how every bartender in town knew his name and he probably needed to make a few changes in his profligate lifestyle.

Early in our friendship Ron also introduced me to a unique nightspot in Cleveland, the Velvet Tango Room, on Abbey and Columbus just west of the Lorain-Carnegie Bridge. It is a world-class establishment—elite, exclusive, and the best place in town for a writer like me to hang out on a stool, checking out the people who walk into the place while I make surreptitious notes, because virtually everyone you've ever heard of in Cleveland eventually winds up there for a nightcap. It's as close as anywhere I've seen in any city to the ambiance and glitter of New York's old Stork Club, and while it's open to anyone who can afford its high-end prices, those wearing tank tops, backward baseball caps, and tacky clothing are encouraged to do their drinking elsewhere. The charming Paulius Nasvytis is the owner and host, and no woman has ever walked into the Tango at night, escorted or not, and left without a red rose from his hand. He even removes the thorns before he distributes the roses.

Outsiders who joke about Cleveland as an in-your-face, spit-on-the-sidewalk town in which etiquette begins and ends with a clean bowling shirt have never been to the Velvet Tango Room—or to Giovanni's, fire (owner chef Doug Katz spells it with a small *f*), Johnny's Bar, and the many other truly fine Cleveland restaurants that make a customer feel pampered like an old and valued friend. I've sent Milan to the Tango several times in the books, even though I doubt such a high-priced bar stocks Stroh's beer—I've never even dared to ask. I'm well aware that it's hardly Milan's kind of place unless he's on an extremely hot date to impress someone, but it's just too "Cleveland" for me not to include it. Everybody should visit the Velvet Tango Room at least once—but make sure you are dressed nicely when you go.

• • •

ALONG WITH THEIR driving directions for getting to Johnny's Bar on that first visit, Rick and Betsy Alexander told me to park across the street in the lot of Saint Rocco's Catholic Church.

I thought they were kidding me! I'd never heard of Saint Rocco. "Saint Rocco" sounded like a made-up name with resonances from old Edward G. Robinson gangster films, a saint whose miracle was rising from the depths of the Cuyahoga River after being buried there with his feet in a block of cement. (Not being a Catholic, I never heard of Saint Colman, either, but that didn't stop me from many years later setting a fictional funeral at Saint Colman's Catholic Church on West 65th Street in *The Best-Kept Secret*. Just as I did with Cleveland itself, and Slovenians, Italians, Browns fans, and the Amish, I've learned a lot about Catholicism since becoming a Clevelander.)

I've visited many houses of worship in and around town, of many different faiths. One I found most interesting was Saint Vitus Church at around East 61st Street, just off St. Clair Avenue. It's in the heart of the Slovenian neighborhood, and I've mentioned several times in my books that Milan Jacovich went to church there when he was a kid and grew up just a few blocks away.

Many of the churches here are pretty old, and while they aren't quite as modern or as comfortable as houses of worship that have been constructed within the past fifteen years, they are awesome to look at. Some are more beautiful inside than they are from the street.

A lot of Catholic parishes in Cleveland cater to certain ethnicities, like Hungarian, Polish, Lithuanian, Italian, and Irish, just to name a few. So many people who found their own ethnic neighborhoods years ago have moved away, out to the suburbs and to bigger and better houses, but they still manage to find their way back to the city every Sunday for services. There are many Baptist churches right in town as well, most of them on the east side, and of course Greater Cleveland has a generous field of churches and synagogues of all faiths. Politicians come to talk to the parishioners a lot, and one of the churches became famous not too long ago when Oprah Winfrey herself came to visit and talk to the crowd.

• • •

THE AVENUE IS the swanky shopping center built about fifteen years ago below our estimable gothic skyscraper, Terminal Tower. At one time railroads stopped there—and the RTA trains still do. You'll find upscale shops, restaurants that run from top-drawer expensive to fast-food quickie, and a spectacular indoor fountain that dances to the piped-in music, including one of my favorites, Aaron Copland's "Appalachian Spring." I wrote about that fountain, and a shoot-out on an escalator, in a climactic moment of the Milan Jacovich adventure, *The Indian Sign.* I was inspired one night, leaving a late movie, when I stopped for about fifteen minutes and watched in awe and lonely splendor as the fountain did its thing to the music when there wasn't a single other spectator in sight. Watching it all by myself was eerily pleasing, and I wondered how I could fit that into a Milan book. Eventually I did.

The Cleveland International Film Festival appears once a year in mid-March for ten days at the downtown theaters in Tower City and draws thousands of people from all over the country. It started small nearly thirty years ago , and it's now one of the larger and more controversial film festivals in America. The Cleveland Film Society runs the festival, and I spent several years serving on its board of trustees, mostly conservative business people who turned out to be fun-loving movie buffs.

A huge wall of windows in the food court very close to the cinema complex provides eaters a place to sit and look out as the Cuyahoga River flows by, especially close to the part of the water I utilized to title *Collision Bend*. It's a great place to have a sandwich or a salad, stake out one of those window tables, and take in the panoramic views both inside and outside of Tower Center. I was at The Avenue one day a few years ago and was walking through the food court when I noticed a woman having her lunch and reading one of my books. That made me feel terrific; I actually had to break her concentration and introduce myself so I could thank her.

The Arcade, between Prospect and Euclid avenues downtown, was one of the first indoor shopping malls built near the turn of the twentieth century and remains a unique public building in America. Hometowners and tourists alike should visit there and take a look, especially since part of it has been transformed into a classy downtown Hyatt Hotel. Some of the suites overlooking the high court have been turned into hotel rooms, too. There are two upscale restaurants and several fast-food joints overlooking the court, plus some eclectic stores, a beauty salon, and a fitness center. Iron tables and chairs are scattered all over the bottom two stories in case you want to grab some lunch, sit back, and enjoy the people. Some are strange indeed, some dress in business suits for their offices just steps away, and every once in a while some beautiful young people in tuxedos and formal dresses show up for a wedding in the hotel, and for the glamorous photo shoot there in the indoor courtyard.

The first time I saw the Arcade, fifteen years ago, I knew I had to include it in one of my books so I could describe the beauty and grace that was designed and built over a hundred years ago, including its vast ceiling made up of hundreds of panes of glass, its filigreed railings and stairways on four different balcony levels, and the clever gargoyles that look down on you from the very top level like those on the Cathedral of Notre Dame in Paris. Indeed, in the climactic scene in *Full*

Cleveland, Milan Jacovich's second literary adventure, somebody gets pitched off the uppermost balcony and lands five stories down on the hard tile floor.

I feel the same respect and awe about the West Side Market. For a hundred years it has anchored Lorain Avenue and West 25th Street with its unmistakable pointed tower, and the very act of buying a pound of potatoes or a string of bratwurst or kielbasa there make me think about the generations of Clevelanders, of every ethnicity and every income range, who have walked its crowded aisles juggling shopping bags and metal carts between the dozens of meat, fish, produce, and specialty stands selling spices, foreign foods, and candy—many of them operated by three and four generations of the same family. There are several amazing bakery stands, too, producing the kind of artisan breads you never find in a supermarket.

Oh yes, and there is another stand that only sells hot sauce with a huge kick—for barbecues or for Mexican or Asian foods. Some of the labels are obscenely named, so I won't mention them. Many items at the stand are so virulently spicy that even people who enjoy spicy foods might actually lose consciousness after taking one small taste.

I visited the West Side Market so often, both in summer and in winter, that eventually I found a way to use it extensively as the setting for several scenes in *The Cleveland Connection*. Even though I haven't mentioned it in a book since, I get a thrill every time I go there to shop. It represents the real, old-time Cleveland like nowhere else in the city. I even did a photo shoot there as I was being interviewed by a now-defunct newspaper about thirteen years back, and the vendor whose produce stall we were blocking in the crowded aisle was very patient with us for about fifteen minutes until he couldn't stand it anymore, and politely but firmly told us he was trying to make some money and that we were very much in the way.

I discovered another place on the near west side just off Lorain Avenue known as Duck Island where I decided to put a murder victim when I was writing the Milan novel *The Best-Kept Secret*. Despite its moniker, it's not an island, and it's not overrun with ducks, either. It's been Duck Island informally for many years because in the old days the kids hanging out on street corners had to "duck" out of sight of cruising cops. Many of the old homes have additions that were rarely built in the same style as the houses themselves, making some of them look like vintage railroad stations in small towns.

I also mentioned a little shop in Duck Island called Haab's Bakery, full of wonderful breads and German pastries—but about a year after that book was published, Haab's closed its doors after holding court for almost a hundred and thirty years. I'd only shopped in there a few times, but its closing broke my heart so much that I wrote a column about it for *Currents*. (Many born-and-bred natives here wax nostalgic about the disappearance of Hough Bakery, which made the most delicious and imaginative cakes anywhere, mostly for birthdays and weddings.) After fifteen years living here, I find myself getting melancholy and nostalgic about the old establishments that finally faded quietly into Cleveland's past.

It has stunned me to learn that people who were born and raised here, or have lived in the area for more than thirty years, have never seen the Arcade or visited the West Side Market. I guess that's akin to the dyed-in-the-wool New Yorkers who have never been to the Statue of Liberty or the Empire State Building. But the Arcade is right downtown with entrances from both Superior and Euclid avenues, and the Market is only five minutes from there, directly across the Lorain-Carnegie Bridge. I urge everyone who hasn't seen both of these remarkable Cleveland places to make a sightseeing trip there as soon

as possible; the experience is unique and the first visit invariably unforgettable. The access is easier here than in New York,
too; after all, to go to the Statue of Liberty you have to take
a *boat*.

●   ●   ●

WHEN I GREW up in Chicago the two major league baseball
clubs, the Cubs and the White Sox, played in two different
parks many miles from each other. They still do today; the
Cubs are the north side team and the White Sox play are on
the south side. The basketball Bulls and the hockey Black
Hawks once held down their territory in the Chicago Stadium
on the west side, and the National Football League team—
who even the well-spoken Chicagoans still refer to as "Da
Bears"—play in Soldier Field right downtown on the shores
of Lake Michigan. In "the Windy City," Soldier Field is even
more blustery in the wintertime than the Cleveland Browns
Stadium. I visited all of them during my Chicago childhood,
and cherish the memories, though I had to go all over town to
enjoy the sports.

In Cleveland it's a lot simpler. It's probably an eight-block
walk, and a brisk one, from Jacobs Field or The Q down to
the edge of Lake Erie, where the Cleveland Browns Football
Stadium was erected in 1999 at the same spot where the old
Cleveland Municipal Stadium stood for almost seventy years.

When I relocated here in December of 1990, one of the first
things I did was attend a Browns game at the old Stadium.
The modern Cleveland Browns Stadium that replaced it is
cleaner and more comfortable and in general a better place
to watch a football game, but I loved the old Stadium. Let's
face it, Jim Brown and Brian Sipe and Paul Warfield played

there, and, in baseball, Bob Feller and Larry Doby and Lou Boudreau. As fine as the new ballpark and football stadium are—Jacobs Field came along a few years earlier than the new Browns football playground—the ghosts of history don't stalk the grass as they used to at the old venue.

The Cleveland Municipal Stadium wasn't nearly as terrific as the new one. There were seventy thousand plus seats which, during years when the Indians weren't very good, were only filled by a handful of die-hard fans for each game. There were places with seats in that stadium where you might find yourself stuck behind a huge pillar around which you could see practically nothing of the actual play. There were far too few rest rooms for women, and the men's rooms, almost twice as many, were grim as could be, even flirting with the city health department as a hazard. I go to both new stadiums these days, even daring to wear a reasonably clean pair of pants—but I still remember the old one with a sense of loss.

As luck would have it, my first in-person Browns game in Cleveland was against the Pittsburgh Steelers, and emotions were running high, despite the subfreezing temperature and a steady drizzle of frozen rain, a phenomenon that almost never happens in Los Angeles. So taken was I with the experience that I set the opening scene of *Deep Shaker* at that very game with Milan and one of his childhood friends, Matt Baznik, in the stands, all bundled up against the cold and rain. Matt was complaining to Milan about the dangers his own teenage son faced, while the painted shirtless fans in the Dawg Pound came close to revolt when star quarterback Bernie Kosar got sacked by the Pittsburgh defense.

It was at least twelve years later that I finally met Kosar in person at a party honoring the Scott Hamilton Cares initiative for the Cleveland Clinic, and I mentioned the book (which he hadn't read) and the scene to him taken from a real game in 1990. Kosar has an amazing memory, both in and out of football. He grinned and said, "We won that game, didn't we?"

•   •   •

ALTHOUGH THIS AREA, like other parts of the country, has plenty of the large chain bookstores like Barnes and Noble and Borders, which carry my books and almost every other author's, I have developed a real emotional connection to the smaller, independent bookshops. I love finding different and out-of-the-way places closer to home, too. In addition to the Fireside Book Shop in Chagrin Falls, I have discovered a few others—decorated in a variety of styles, generally managed by their owners behind the counter, and much friendlier than the chain stores. Just like any of its super sisters, an independent store can order any book you may want from anywhere.

Here are some of my favorites. Named after a genteel English film, 84 Charing Cross, on Detroit Road, is only eight minutes from downtown Cleveland and just downstairs from the Cleveland Public Theater, selling mostly used books. It is a lovely, almost-British type establishment that smells wonderfully of musty and sometimes rare volumes.

On Coventry Road in Cleveland Heights, Mac's Backs is one of the most durable bookstores in town, carrying some fascinating new and used books. It's connected to Tommy's right next door, a health food restaurant, also around for many years, that draws enormous crowds for the kind of lunches and dinners you'll never in a million years find in Manhattan.

As a matter of fact, Coventry Road itself, just about eight blocks from where I live, has quite a history. Over the years it's been home and haven for beatniks, hippies, motorcycle gangs, punks, rockers, and hip-hop. Its crowd is eclectic, eats at Tommy's and Hunan Coventry and The Inn on Coventry, and includes just about all the teenagers one can find on any given street, many of them sporting purple-dyed Mohawk haircuts, tattoos, and visible (and painful-looking) face piercings. It also brings out classic-movie lovers who can find their vintage material at VidStar Video right on the corner. Peppered throughout this crowd—perfect for those who enjoy "people watching"—are the fresh-faced young mothers with their preschoolers and even the occasional grandma and grandpa, too.

All these small, comfortable stores have personalities that the more efficient and far larger establishments can't seem to capture. The Northrop Book Store in Olmsted Falls is another one.

A booksigning at Northrop brought me to picturesque Olmsted Falls for the first time in my life, despite the fact it's so close by—only about ten minutes south of I-480. Olmsted Falls feels like a small town a hundred miles from nowhere. The bookshop is nestled among many other stores and restaurants in a quaint retail section in which one can spend the entire afternoon browsing. Sometimes a train running on the tracks just a few yards away makes a hell of a noise, shakes the building in which you're standing, and gets everyone's attention. I asked Gail Rapps, the local book dealer, about the actual falls in Olmsted Falls and learned that from the road you can't see them because years ago someone built a house in front of the scenic vista. There are walking paths galore to get to it, though, including one just behind the Olmsted Falls Library.

Olmsted Falls is the hometown of another dear friend, Sherri Robertson, who was married to the famous local resident Don Robertson, author and journalist. Unfortunately, when I arrived here in 1990 Don was very ill, and I never got to meet him. I met Sherri after Don's passing, and we have since become good friends, sharing great stories and common passions like music, literature, and movies.

A local gentleman from a nearby town, who, I heard, stops into Northrop Books almost every day just to chat, told me in no uncertain terms that I should write a Milan Jacovich book—and he's never read any of them, by the way—entitled *Strongsville*. South of Cleveland, Strongsville is a nice suburban city I've visited several times, but it's just not a very good title for a mystery novel. Strongsville sounds more like a name for a Marvel Comics book about the Fantastic Four.

Though I might send Milan down to Olmsted Falls to solve a fictional murder. That's a pretty little town with a *lot* of personality. You never know who, what, or where may find its way into one of my books. That's one of the great joys of being a writer: taking Greater Cleveland and its suburbs and towns in, and then churning it back out again—on paper.

CHAPTER 6

"You're a Strange Person"

ALL THROUGH MY years of living in Cleveland Heights, my next-door neighbors have been Skip and Carrie Chizmar, who have now moved down to Florida. Neighbors just don't get any better. We didn't really hang out together; we were never kaffeeklatsch neighbors, we never barbecued or drank beer in our attached backyards or borrowed one another's tools—as if I had any tools to borrow! They were a married couple with four teenaged daughters when I moved in, and Skip was a glutton for yard work, while I was a bachelor who worked at home in my second-floor office and didn't relish unexpected company during the day, and who hired somebody to come over and take care of my lawn. But we'd always chat out on the front grass, and whenever I left town on a book tour or vacation, Carrie was marvelous about coming over to collect my mail, and to feed and play with my cat, too. Fortunately she was also a cat person, and had a big black Tom named King, who was fond of sitting in the window and checking out the action on the street.

Once, while I was on a trip to California, burglars busted into my home through a window and Skip came over and boarded it up until I could get home to replace it. Carrie was a fanatic over elephants—not the real ones who eat peanuts, but elephant dolls and paintings and figurines. She had a collection in her home that must have numbered in the hundreds—and whenever I was gone for a few days I'd always find her a little wooden or brass elephant from whatever town I was visiting as a thank-you token for cat-sitting.

About a year after I moved in, we were talking one day and she remarked that sometimes when she was awake at three or four in the morning to take one of her daughters to ice skating practice—and don't ask me why children skate in the middle of the night because, to me it's one of those vast unsolved mysteries—she'd notice the light on in my office and she'd see me bent over my computer keyboard in my second-floor sunroom, or maybe just wandering around in my living room. "You're a strange person, Les," she said.

It made me laugh, but I readily admit it's true in certain ways. Everyone I know who makes a living in the arts has got to be a little peculiar, because nobody in their right mind would volunteer to live this way. It's the most financially insecure business in the world, and for every Julia Roberts (no relation), who earns twenty million dollars per picture, or Stephen King or John Grisham or Dean Koontz, who could easily pay off my house mortgage with what they carry in their pockets, there are thousands of other painters, writers, actors, dancers, and sculptors who squeak by from one payday to the next—and those paydays are rarely regular. Even those artists most people might consider "famous" whose names frequently appear in newspapers and on television occasionally wonder from whence the next sack of groceries will come.

It's no surprise that eventually we turn into strange people with eccentric ways and sometimes inexplicable peculiarities.

Thomas Wolfe, who was quite tall, wrote on a yellow pad placed on top of his refrigerator where he stood all day long. When he was done with a page of, say, *Look Homeward, Angel*, he'd rip it off the pad and toss it onto the floor, then continue writing. It was up to his secretary to collect all the pages, which he never numbered, and sort them out at the end of the day.

Ernest Hemingway, who was completely undisciplined about everything else in his life, arose faithfully at four or five each morning and wrote undisturbed until noon, at which time he abandoned his labors for his other passions—women, fishing, boxing, bullfighting, and drinking. Whatever eccentricities he allowed to carry him through the rest of the day and evening, he was still okay and ready to write again the next morning. His house in Havana—the only place in Cuba set aside to honor a United States citizen—is famous for its tribe of six-toed cats, which may or may not have anything to do with Papa's peculiarities.

Lawrence Block, one of the best and most prolific mystery writers in America, goes for months without putting a single word on paper, and then hides away at a writer's retreat or an out-of-the-way hotel for six or eight weeks and turns out astonishing crime fiction like *The Burglar Who Thought He Was Bogart* or *A Dance At the Slaughterhouse*. Other authors prefer to haul their laptops out to someplace intensely public, like a Starbucks or McDonald's or even the food court of a shopping mall or a park bench, and do their writing there.

Two of the top private eye writers in America, Loren D. Estleman and Bill Pronzini, both write their books on manual typewriters, secure in the belief that the energy it takes to pound those old keys is translated onto the paper. Loren, who actually collects old typewriters, has never been known to touch a computer, or even an IBM Selectric, and if I want to contact him by e-mail I simply write to his wife, author Deborah Morgan, and he leans over her shoulder to read it. Pronzini's wife, best-selling author Marcia Muller, does her typing on the unused backs of other manuscript pages rather than throwing them away. Waste not, want not, I suppose.

•   •   •

THERE IS A best-selling author of my acquaintance who lives in California and routinely pulls in an advance of several million dollars per book. Every morning when she wakes up, she puts on a crisp, ironed blouse, a skirt, hose and high heels, and full makeup, and walks from her bedroom to her office twenty feet away. Then she types all day in splendid isolation, writing marvelous British tales of murder and suspense. She feels more professional, she says, when she gets dressed up to work.

Noted Irish film director Terence Young (*Wait Until Dark*, *From Russia With Love*, etc.), with whom I became friendly in the late seventies while we were both in Hong Kong working on separate film productions, always wore a long-sleeved shirt and a tie when he was directing a movie, even if it was being filmed on location in one of the hottest and most humid jungles in the world. All dressed up, Terence felt he got more respect and admiration from the cast and crew who always looked up to him.

Most authors, unlike my Southern California colleague with the high heels and full makeup, dress casually for their writing sessions. Novelist and poet Kate Braverman once said that if you're planning to write a novel, prepare to spend the next two years in your bathrobe, and she's absolutely correct. Even though most people in Cleveland are used to seeing me in sports jackets or suits and ties, and sometimes in sweaters, I virtually *live* my work week in blue jeans, T-shirts, or sweats. My decision making about what outfit to wear on a given working day hinges solely upon what happens to be clean at the time. If I were ever to wear a tie into my office, I doubt if I could get my computer to boot up, because it wouldn't recognize me.

Although I scribble notes almost anywhere I happen to be, I like to do the actual writing in my office when there's no one else home. When they were young, my children were thoroughly trained to bother me when I was working only if they happened to be on fire. I can zero in on what I'm doing much better without any distractions. My writing time is the part of the day when the only noise I want in the house is a great classical music CD, or when I'm rewriting or researching, perhaps some melodic jazz. More often the only music I'll hear is the sound of myself as I hum or whistle while I work. I like having all my "stuff" within arm's reach—my reference books, my pens and pencils, the photographs of my loved ones framed all around the room. I even keep my mug warmer handy to insure that the eight or ten cups of tea I drink every day are always hot and delicious. For most of my life I was a coffee-aholic, drinking a minimum of a pot and a half every day, and often another cup or two in the evening, but since I switched to tea a few years back I haven't missed the coffee, because I still get to drink my hot beverages.

When I first moved into this house I not only wrote, but spent most of my time in the second-floor sunroom that serves as my office, reading or talking on the telephone. There are three other upstairs bedrooms, and on the main floor a living room, dining room, kitchen, and another sunroom where I keep my one and only television set. That's because I don't watch much television—I'm often too busy at night to bother with it, and during the day it isn't that hard to avoid meaningless, stupid "entertainment" like all the soap operas featuring beautiful but boring "actors," and of course the imbecilic Jerry Springer Show.

In the wintertime the branches of the trees outside my window are skeleton bare and dark brown, standing solidly against the pewter gray of the sky. In the spring and summer those trees become an almost impenetrable screen of several shades of green, sparkling in the sunlight. The squirrels do acrobatics on my electric wires, the blue jays and the crows are raucous and aggressive, and the bright red cardinals—I learned later that they are the official state bird of Ohio—absolutely tear my attention away from everything with their colors. But I still write.

My second-floor office looks out on Cain Park, but it's a lot more than just a park to walk through. There are tennis courts and a playground. There is an art gallery that I can see through the trees from my back windows. There are two theaters—a major amphitheater which presents a musical every summer, along with an entire raft of concerts by some internationally famous performers—and a smaller more intimate three-quarter-round theater which also presents a musical and concerts that attract a smaller audience. Every July an entire three-day weekend is given over to the Cain Park Arts Festival, with almost one hundred painters, sculptors, and arts and crafts experts who spread their tents on both sides of the main sidewalk nearly the length of the park itself. It draws several thousand people. I'll take a walk down there to look around and invariably meet ten or twenty people I know.

During the Arts Festival the street in front of my house is clogged with cars parking, or trying to park, from morning till night, and if it isn't too hot I get a kick out of sitting up on my second-floor deck watching people arrive and depart from their tour of the Arts Festival. Invariably when a couple arrives, the passenger jumps out and directs the driver into a narrow parking space so the car won't block the access to a residential driveway—like mine. If I might want to go somewhere during that time, I don't even dare try to back my car out for fear of being clobbered by someone looking desperately for a parking place.

For me, the best part of Cain Park is during the winter, after a snowstorm. A steep hill running from the surface of Taylor Road down into the park collects hard-packed snow on its slope, and brings out more youthful sledders than anywhere else in the city. Some slide down like sledding aficionados, while others belly flop joyfully. I'm far too old to go rocketing down that incline on a sled, or even an old tire, but I like to stop and watch; the local families with their children and their cold-reddened noses, resemble those Norman Rockwell used to paint more than fifty years ago.

● ● ●

SINCE MOVING TO Cleveland, and even before, while I was still working on my novels in Los Angeles, my day has almost always been the same. I wake up before eight o'clock in the morning. I make my tea and drink it while sitting out on my balcony—when the weather is decent, that is—reading the newspaper. (I had a tiny balcony in my Los Angeles flat, facing east to embrace the cool morning sun—now my house in Cleveland Heights has a second-floor deck ten times as large, and it too faces east.) I always have a pad of paper and a pen or pencil handy so I can jot down interesting stuff that I find in the paper, either on the front page or sometimes hidden away on the inside.

Mostly I make no more than small notes that I file away and stew about for a while, until I either become inspired to explore further or I get bored with the idea and forget about it. Some of them came from full-blown articles on the front page of the *Plain Dealer*, and wind up as the linchpin of an entire novel, like the news report of a con game I tossed around in my head for weeks before I turned it into *The Irish Sports Pages*. I'm always thinking about the next book.

Then with the newspaper finally read for the day, I go inside to my office and begin my own labors. Some of that labor is intense.

The first thing I always do is read over the work I did the day before, tightening and changing, cutting out some extra padding, and sometimes adding more material. That always gets me up to speed.

Until the advent of caller ID, I would never answer my phone before three o'clock in the afternoon, allowing my voice mail to pick up the messages. That's why the majority of professional authors prefer working early in the morning, like Hemingway, before the mail carrier arrives with all those irritating bills to be paid and before the telephone starts to ring, breaking their creative concentration and taking little bites out of their psychic butt.

E-mail, although a convenience, can really demand much of my time, which I'd rather spend putting words to paper. I do get some nice e-mails from fans who read my books and want to tell me all about themselves—but I can only answer them politely and briefly in three or four sentences, showing my appreciation (after all, they keep me in business) and then getting back to my craft. Longer electronic messages, or phone calls, I return to fewer people than I can count on one hand—and two of them are Valerie and Darren, my children.

A lot of people, most of whom I've never met, send a letter or message, or phone me, and tell me they're in the throes of writing a manuscript and would I please take eight or nine hours out of my life to read it and then write a long critique for them. I always tell them I'm behind them one hundred percent in spirit, but I just don't have the inclination to read and critique somebody else's novel. If I did that for everybody, I'd have very little time left to do what I need to do, which is to write my own books.

Before many of us put our numbers on the Do Not Call list of telephone salespeople who bother the hell out of us during dinnertime and attempt to sell us dance lessons or a funeral plot, I wouldn't answer the phone between five thirty and eight p.m., either. I still never answer the phone before three unless I'm on a work break or I can glance down at the caller ID and see if it's someone I want or need to talk to.

However, during my entire adult life, including my Hollywood days when I was the producer and head writer of such network television shows as *The Hollywood Squares* and *It Takes Two* on NBC as well as the later Cleveland days when I became a full-time novelist and critic, I've *always* had my home phone number listed in the telephone book.

Sometimes I'll get ten or more pages done in a day, but other times I'll spend six or seven frustrating hours staring at the computer screen and coming up with only a single paragraph. It's much harder squeezing out that one paragraph than zipping through those ten pages.

We've all reached that point in a project where we know exactly where we want to go, but haven't the foggiest notion of how to get there. I wouldn't dignify it by calling it "writer's block," because as Norman Mailer observed, writing comes out of the ego, and writer's block is simply a failure of ego—but I have no problem calling it a *stumbling* block. At least three-quarters of the mystery writers I know admit to the problem. Every writer in the world suffers it from time to time, from the first-timers penning their hopeful debut novels at five o'clock in the morning to the seasoned veterans like me, with twenty-three books to my credit.

Quite often I keep on working right up until dinnertime. After that I may read a book I'm reviewing for the *Plain Dealer* or for *Currents,* or on occasion for the *Washington Post Book World* or some other national newspaper. Once in a while I sit back and escape into a mystery. I manage to read somewhere between one hundred and one hundred twenty books a year. About half are mystery novels, either ones I review myself, or those written by friends like Dennis Lehane, Robert Crais, Marcia Muller, Robert J. Randisi, and Margaret Maron. Another ten or fifteen are novels that have nothing to do with murder and mayhem, and frequently include the great classics I've read and loved several times throughout my life. *The Great Gatsby*, *Moby-Dick*, *Huckleberry Finn*, and *The Sun Also Rises* are novels I reread every five or six years. The rest of my reading is nonfiction—history, biography, politics, or current events.

I frequently have at least two volumes open and ready on my desk, but they're never the same type of book. I especially get confused when I'm reading more than one mystery at a time.

I do a lot more with my life than read. Every few days I have to go out to buy groceries and cleaning stuff for the house. There are nights I'll have a party or a dinner or a show to attend. Because, when all is said and done, I don't ever hide away like a hermit at home. I enjoy the people and the places in my city. I'm very sociable, and I live like everyone else.

But when I'm in the middle of writing a novel, which is almost all the time, no matter what I'm doing or where I am, a part of my head is always in that book, every moment. Doctors, lawyers, Indians' outfielders, plumbers, and everyone else who works for a living leaves their job at the office or ballpark each night and goes home to relax or out on the town to play. But authors never *ever* stop writing completely. It's just a part of how we're put together.

•   •   •

THE WAY I feel about publicity is that if anyone wants to say good things about my books, that's great! Anything else— anything too personal—and they're on shaky ground. Don't get me wrong, I like being out and about—*Cleveland Magazine* once characterized me some years ago among the "often seen" when I used to go out nearly every night. I'd be a liar if I said I don't love it when people come up to me in restaurants or on the street and tell me they like my work, even if it takes less than a minute. But I cherish my privacy even more. It's murder for me to have to shave and look presentable every time I want to run to the supermarket or to fill up the car with now obscenely expensive gasoline.

So yes, I do prowl around in the middle of the night sometimes. Mostly it's because of the 45-minute rule. If I'm in bed and can't seem to get to sleep, I give myself forty-five minutes in which to try, and then I get up and do something relatively useful, which is usually writing or reading. I've reached that age where one doesn't like to waste a single minute, so staring fixedly at the ceiling in my bedroom all night holds no allure— I memorized it years ago. Similarly, when Milan stays awake at night and worries about his case or his love life, he studies a crack in his bedroom ceiling that looks like a map of Brazil.

Sometimes, though, I'll pick the dark times to do my research on the city of Cleveland. At night there is generally little traffic, and I can slow down or even stop and dictate into my tape recorder whatever information I need about a specific neighborhood or even a street corner. Every so often a zone car will cruise along and ask me what I'm doing, as it looks for all the world like I'm checking out a place to rob—so I always make sure I carry a copy of one of my books in the car on my late-night reconnaissance missions so they'll believe I'm researching a novel and not setting up a heist.

Once, when I'd been living here only a few months, I left the house at 1:30 a.m. to scout out the perfect spot to dump a corpse. I drove around for a while, thinking of *The Cleveland Connection*, which I was writing, and wound up down on Woodland Avenue in the east thirties, where I found what I was looking for—right in the middle of the city, a place where a body wouldn't be noticed for several days. Nobody had told me that Woodland Avenue wasn't the smartest place to go in the middle of the night, and the following day a friend observed that I was damn lucky the dumped body didn't wind up being mine. I even spent two hours one late evening driving around the near west side checking out where prostitutes roam on the streets.

I refuse to succumb to urban paranoia. I know people in the Cleveland suburbs, both east and west, who wouldn't dream of coming downtown after dark, which effectively shuts them out of orchestra and rock concerts, great theater and music, art gallery openings, and Major League baseball and basketball, as well as some of the area's best and most interesting restaurants and saloons and nightspots. It's their loss, but it's Cleveland's, too, because we depend on the denizens of the suburbs as much as they depend on us—whether they like to admit it or not.

While I'm not so stupid as to walk some of our town's meaner streets wearing a Rolex and flashing a roll of fifties, I still believe that careful and sensible people never run into trouble in the nighttime city. That's why God made locks on car doors. Besides, I've never had a roll of fifties to flash, rarely carrying more than thirty dollars in my pocket, and my most expensive watch cost $69.95.

• • •

I PROBABLY GET anywhere from fifteen to twenty jolts of inspiration of one sort or another on any given day, which is why I always carry a notebook with me, whether I'm wearing a suit, a tuxedo, a casual sweater and chinos, or as is most often the case, jeans or sweats. I drag that notebook with me to formal dinners, to Giant Eagle for groceries, or even when I take a walk through Cain Park, just out my back door. And there is always a mini-tape recorder in my car so I can record an idea without my eyes leaving the road. Plot ideas are a dime a dozen; it's actually writing the damn book that's the hard part.

That's why it never ceases to amuse me when perfect strangers approach me and proceed to spin a half-formed plot for a new Milan book, many times including the plea that they wish to collaborate with me. Sometimes they call me on the phone; more often they e-mail, they approach me while I'm doing a signing, and once in a while they even show up unannounced on my doorstep. That was the case a few years ago with one gentleman who actually stopped me coming down my front steps at six thirty in the morning when I was taking a very sick cat to the vet. He assured me that he was a former neighbor from across the street (I couldn't remember him for the life of me), and he wanted to collaborate on an idea for a mystery novel.

Good idea, pal, but please listen carefully: *I don't collaborate.*

In my former life as a TV writer I was often forced to work with other writers, mostly in the comedy field. On my very first network television job in New York, *Candid Camera*, the late Allen Funt—I still have nightmares about the weeks I spent working for him, one of the meanest bosses I've ever known—barely greeted me on my first morning at his office before sending me off to a small room (which he had secretly wired so that at any time he could flip a switch and listen to whether or not our typewriters were clacking) to sit across the desk from a writer I'd never met before and told both of us, "Be funny." I wasn't really that surprised, because most television comedy writers work with a partner, sometimes even by choice. Many playwrights, like George S. Kaufman and Moss Hart, also worked well together.

Not novelists.

With the possible exception of *Mutiny on the Bounty*, written by Charles Nordhoff and James Norman Hall, or *Fail Safe* by William J. Wheeler and Eugene Burdick, I'm hard-pressed to think of any other really successful novels that were cowritten. *The Brothers Karamazov* by Fyodor Dostoevsky and Irving Lipnik? *The Great Gatsby* by F. Scott Fitzgerald and Ed Henderson? Or even the crackling hard-boiled mystery, *I, the Jury* by Mickey Spillane and Seamus J. Kelly? I think not. Novel writers are usually out of contact with everyone except the closest of friends and family while they write. When the story character reveals something important and secret, it actually originates from the person writing it, and comes both from the gut and the heart, and not from kicking ideas around with a collaborator who's never written a word before in his or her life.

Most people who want to work with me on a novel really want to spend five minutes telling me their story and then go away while I labor alone for six or eight months writing the book. Oh, and by the way, they'd also like to split the book money with me, 50-50.

Sure, like *that's* going to happen. As I said, I get multiple ideas of my own every day, and I don't need a shadow at my elbow telling me where to put my commas.

Besides that, if I work on one of my own ideas and complete a novel that gets published, I'm paid all the money—the advance and the royalties that follow for many years. On the other hand, if I collaborate with someone else, even someone who pulls his or her own writing weight, I'd have to split the profits with them right from the beginning. That doesn't work for me. Do the math.

Someone actually tried to convince me to let her collaborate with me on this memoir I'm writing now—for no money and no credit. She just wanted me to thank her profusely. She seemed to think she knew Cleveland better than I did. Perhaps she does—and she's welcome to write her *own* memoir.

This one's *mine*.

Fiction writing is by its very nature a solitary and sometimes lonely profession. There's no one to hang out with at the coffee machine and bang creative ideas back and forth, no one to run over to at the next cubicle and share inspiration, and—thank God—there are no meetings. The forced "meeting" is one of the main reasons that network television is so bland, uninspired, and downright bad; it's no accident that people describe a camel as a horse designed by a committee.

A novel, on the other hand, is the most intensely personal and private thing one can do while completely dressed, and the day I collaborate on writing a book with anyone—including a family member, a loved one, or even an author more well-known than I am—is the day I hang it up altogether and find a different line of work.

When my son, Darren, was about nineteen or so and we were still living in Los Angeles, we were out to lunch one day, and he began a conversation with "When you die . . ."

Yikes. That's a pretty tough subject for any offspring to handle, and even harder for a parent to hear. For a moment it killed my appetite. "When you die," he went on, "I'm going to start writing books about Milan Jacovich Junior."

Milan Junior, in all of my books, was the older of the two boys of the private investigator, the other being Stephen. It never occurred to me to write a novel with him as the protagonist. And the idea of someone else writing a book about him, even Darren, left a peculiar taste in my mouth.

"If I *do* die and you start writing about Milan Junior," I said to him, "I'll come back and haunt you and clang my chains in your ear. Get your own book to write, if you have to; the Jacovich family is *mine.*"

There just aren't many children who follow their parents into the book-writing business. Actors, maybe, or musicians. Not writers. Not many, anyway; only Alexandre Dumas *père et fils,* come to mind, along with Peter Benchley, the author of *Jaws*, whose grandfather, Robert Benchley, was one of the wittiest and most sophisticated writers in the first half of the twentieth century. I'd be thrilled to death if Darren or Valerie ever decided to write books, and I'd do everything within my power to help them succeed—as long as they weren't writing more of *my* books.

Over the years I've taught or given symposiums on writing at several local venues, including Notre Dame College, Case Western Reserve University, Cuyahoga Community College, the Cleveland Heights Recreation Department, the twice yearly Lakeland Writers Conference, and the Poets and Writers League of Greater Cleveland. I really enjoy teaching writing, because I think I learn more myself than do my students.

Whenever I teach a class in fiction writing or screenwriting, I always look at the eager and anxious wannabe authors and begin with the same phrase: "What are you doing here? Why aren't you home right now, *writing*?"

Going to class or hearing a lecture about writing is just fine, and when I'm up there delivering it I try to make it a bit entertaining as well. But the truth is, you'll get a lot more done by bending your brain and your backbone toward the work at hand and forgetting about all the minutiae of your daily life.

Sure, there are dishes to wash, socks to launder, perhaps the grass to cut or the bathroom floor to mop. In addition, you have to think about calling your mom to chat and set up a dinner at her house over the weekend. You need to check in with your spouse or significant other, or your friends who had suggested going out for buffalo wings and dancing next Friday night. You have groceries to buy, too, a three-thousand mile oil change and tune-up for your car, and you can't forget about those bills that have to be paid every month.

I understand that. All of us have other things to do.

But if you want to write—if you want to put what's important on the page, if you want to become a real author whether or not anyone has offered to publish you—you must banish all those other things from your mind and get to work!

It's nice to put in six or eight hours at the typewriter or computer daily, the way I do—but more often than not you have a job other than writing so you can pay the bills. Fine, then set aside one hour every day for writing. Just one hour. Get up an hour early in the morning, or go to bed an hour later at night. Skip television—there's little on anymore except stupid reality shows—or even skip breakfast. Maybe in that hour you can get an entire page written. Good for you. Feel proud of yourself and do it again the next day.

And the next day after that.

At the end of a year, chances are you'll have completed the first draft of an actual *book*.

All the years I lived in Los Angeles, as a producer and writer, I rarely got questions from newbies just starting out. They probably phoned about five thousand producers and thirty thousand writers before they got around to me. Whenever I went out to dinner, I'd have to check out the server who came to my table—if they were beautiful they were trying to become a model or an actor, and if they weren't so spectacular-looking, they would probably rush home after their shift to write a screenplay or a novel. Everybody wanted to be Somebody in Los Angeles—no questions asked.

Things are different in Cleveland, and I answer those questions nearly every day of my life.

Once many years ago I chatted with a woman at a writer's conference who told me that she'd been studying and researching her not-yet-written novel for the past *eight years*! She mentioned that she had spent two entire weeks trying to discover the exact type of chemicals added to the swimming pools in the backyards of houses in a certain part of town—different from chemicals added in another town. I was too kind to tell her that after wasting all that time looking up abstruse facts and doing research, she would probably just continue to avoid ever writing the book.

Having written twenty-three books so far—twenty-four if you count this one—I can tell you that the writing itself is everything. Even the people who are closest to me have to understand if suddenly, in the middle of a conversation or the middle of the night, I get a flash of inspiration and run off to write—or at least to make notes, because writing a book is not like digging ditches or making sausages. It's cerebral and visceral, woven into the fabric of my being and with me always—twenty-four hours a day.

As I've said, with the exception of some superstars—TV people like Oprah, movie stars like Tom Cruise and Jack Nicholson, and writers like Stephen King and Mary Higgins Clark—virtually everybody in the arts is always living from day to day or from paycheck to paycheck, especially writers, who get an advance from their publisher for a new book, then wait at least six months, and often more than that, for the royalties. I'd rather live that way, as I've done all my life, than go to an office every day and work diligently for somebody else. It's what I chose when I was extremely young. When I was acting on stage, producing and writing television shows, teaching writing, and even, for ten years, playing piano and singing in a remarkable number of restaurants, nightclubs and gin joints in Los Angeles, I always lived the same way and enjoyed what I did. I was just fine with the light side of the money, as long as I was enjoying the heavy side of what I do best.

Today's athletes make dizzying salaries and promotion money, many of them earning multimillions every year, and several thousand each and every time they pick up a baseball bat or a basketball. Good for them, too—but I remember when I was a kid that some of the biggest stars in baseball, football, and basketball earned paychecks somewhere between ten and thirty thousand dollars a year. It was decent money even back then, but hardly outrageous. The athletes were tickled pink to get it, because it was never about money—it was about doing what they loved.

Writers are the same way.

I'm thrilled to death that the author of the Harry Potter books, J. K. Rowling, has finally become the first *billionaire* in writing history, who now has even more money than Elizabeth II of Great Britain. As I pointed out to someone about Rowling's earnings, that's more than I earn in a month.

A handful of American writers like King and Mary Higgins Clark and Anne Rice have hit the best-seller lists time and again, and have pocketed millions. I take my hat off to all of them. But I also applaud the other authors who belong to the larger group of "mid-list writers," and who earn just enough to pay their bills with little left over for luxuries. They have decided writing is more important to them than money.

I salute them—because I'm one of them.

CHAPTER 7

Milan and Me

I'VE BEEN WRITING private eye mystery novels since 1986. Six of them starred my Los Angeles actor/investigator Saxon, and thirteen of them were about Milan Jacovich, who has been called "Cleveland's Favorite Private Eye." I admit Milan is *my* favorite private eye, too (along with Raymond Chandler's immortal Philip Marlowe in such classics as *The Big Sleep* and *Farewell, My Lovely*). Over the last eighteen years I've gotten to know him pretty well, and have come to like him a great deal—his faults and all. He spends chunks of every day with me—in my mind and on paper—and I know him inside and out.

However, he's not me.

Over the years some loyal readers have wanted to know all about me, but I believe they're actually asking about Milan. This may come as a great shock to you, but I am not much like the fictional character at all. I'd like to take this chapter to explain the differences—and maybe a few of the similarities—between Milan Jacovich and me.

Milan Jacovich lives in Cleveland Heights, and so do I—but not in the same place. First of all, I began writing the Milan books before I ever moved here, and secondly I would have to be insane to use my own address as his, where everyone in the world could read it—including people I don't know—and possibly stop by to chat for a while. I get enough nut cases knocking on my front door as it is.

Milan Jacovich was born in Cleveland, and except for a tour in Vietnam in the last days of the war, during the early seventies, he has always lived in the neighborhood. I, on the other hand, was born in Chicago, and lived in New York, Augusta, Georgia, and Los Angeles, with shorter stays in Hong Kong, Detroit, Cleveland, and once again Chicago before I moved here permanently. When I get nostalgic over the joys and adventures of my childhood, Chicago comes to mind, not Cleveland.

Milan's parents were named Louis and Mirijanna, and were both born in Ljublana, Slovenia. They immigrated to this country sometime after the Second World War and settled in the Slovenian neighborhood just off St. Clair Avenue in the east sixties. Dad Louis worked in the steel mills for his entire life. I never wrote about Milan's grandparents, and never really thought about them while crafting my novels, although I'm sure they lived and died in Slovenia. Both Milan's parents passed away before I started writing his story, and in the books I never really discussed when or how. Frankly, I don't even know.

My parents, like Milan's, died relatively early in my life. My father's name was Lester, and he was born in London within the sound of the Bow Bells, so he had a wickedly charming Cockney accent. He ran away from home when he was fifteen and toured all over England working as a laborer with a circus—the stuff of which movies should be made! When he got back to London his family had gone to America. His father was dead by then, but his mother and five siblings pretty much left the British Isles without him, and although I have a vague memory of seeing my paternal grandmother when I was two years old, I never really knew her. Lester, only sixteen, made sufficient money as a London boxer—until he was matched against the first-ranking featherweight challenger of Britain and got knocked on his ass for the first and last time. He collected his saved money and paid his own way to the United States. He went to college and to dental school at the University of Chicago, and became one of the best-known dentists in the city.

My mother, Eleanor, was born in New York City and her sister, my aunt Cecile, was born in Chicago two years earlier. The whole family moved back to Illinois when they were still children. Although her parents were both from Europe—her mother from Germany and her father from Rumania—all her life she spoke perfect English. She was one of the funniest people I ever knew, though in a quiet way—she whispered all her jokes, and they were even more comical *sotto voce* than spoken out loud. Her father, Jack, was the only grandparent I ever really got to know; he was a clothing salesman who worked all over the country from the east coast to Minnesota and the rest of the Midwest, and eventually he retired to a little apartment in Hollywood, California. Years later, when I saw the Broadway version of *The Music Man*, the leading character, Professor Harold Hill, reminded me of my grandfather.

My father died from a massive heart attack when I was thirteen, and my mother died almost exactly twenty years later from cancer. Now, my family is no more a current subject for me in real life than Milan's is for him in fiction. However, we share one more familial truth besides both of us losing our parents when we were young: neither of us has brothers or sisters.

Milan's fictional wife, Lila, divorced him just before the series started and had already moved in with a man named Joe Bradac, a guy they both knew from high school and who Milan genially detested. My former wife, Gail, never moved in with anyone at all until twenty-four years after we divorced, just two years before she died. (She used to say that the marriage was a disaster but the divorce was a roaring success.)

Readers all ask me about my two sons, just like Milan's. In my first Cleveland novel, *Pepper Pike*, Milan Junior was about twelve years old and Stephen was five, and they have spent some time on the pages of almost every book since. I don't *have* two sons—rather one child of each gender, Valerie and Darren. They are now older than Milan's kids, and though they read my novels, they don't relate to either of the boys. Milan Junior is a talented football player, a wide receiver; Valerie was a competitive swimmer, and Darren was much more into baseball and volleyball as a teenager.

Milan smokes Winston cigarettes. I learned early in my Milan-writing career that many Slovenians smoke—and many favor Winston. I've never been a cigarette smoker, and the few times I did have one, I never inhaled—just like Bill Clinton. I did, however, smoke a pipe from the time I was fifteen until about four years ago when I gave it up overnight. I'd be hard-pressed to find anyone who smokes a pipe nowadays—I think it began falling out of fashion when Andy Hardy's father, the judge, stopped smoking pipes in the old movies. I only smoke two or three cigars a year, usually over lunch or dinner with male friends, because most women that I know loathe the smell of them.

In the early part of my lifetime almost everyone I knew smoked, including both my parents and my former wife—but today, when many more people have thankfully grown smart about the dangers of tobacco, I hardly know anyone who smokes. And because almost everywhere you go in this modern day is mandated a "smoke-free environment," it's just not a common sight anymore.

If you don't smoke cigarettes at all, kissing someone who does tastes like kissing an ashtray. I like it better this new and informed way.

Milan Jacovich drinks Stroh's Beer—bottle, no glass—and he drinks a lot of them in every book, again because I learned early that Stroh's is the beer of choice for most Slovenians in the Cleveland area. For some reason almost every one of my readers thinks I drink Stroh's, too, and several have offered to buy me one. But they couldn't be more off the mark, because I've never had a Stroh's in my life.

In fact, I'm not much of a beer drinker at all, but if I'm having it, I always order either an imported beer or one from a microbrewery, mostly the good ones like Great Lakes Brewing Company and Willoughby Brewing Company here in the Cleveland area. I enjoy a good wine—almost always red—but prefer spirits, especially single malt Scotch. The best I've ever had is Laphroaig (pronounced La-FROYG), from Islay, in Scotland, tasting of smoke and peat moss, and I freely admit Laphroaig is an acquired taste.

I'm also fond of Dalwhinnie and several other single malt Scotches when I can't get served the one I love, and on rare occasions I'll sip on a good bourbon whiskey—either with no ice at all or just a teaspoonful of water to bring out the subtle flavors. As I've stated earlier, I'm particularly partial to gin martinis before dinner, and after a great meal I like to toy with a balloon of cognac or, even better, an Armagnac—both types of French brandy.

But unlike Milan, I don't believe I'll ever be a Stroh's drinker. As President George H. W. Bush used to say about all sorts of things: "Not gonna happen."

If Milan isn't sitting in his living room drinking Stroh's, he's out having a few, usually at Vuk's Tavern near East 55th Street and St. Clair. He had his first legal drink in Vuk's tav-

ern and has maintained a lifelong relationship with the owner
and bartender, Vuk—named Louis Vukovich by his mother
but known to his friends and patrons by the shorter version.
Milan goes into Vuk's when he's lonely or whenever he needs
to slide an idea past the stoic and mustachioed bartender, or
just when he wants to sit and drink a beer and watch the Indians' game on TV with people he knows rather than sulking by
himself in his quiet apartment.

I rarely drink alone the way he does—never at home and
hardly ever in a saloon anymore. When I have a drink with
friends it could be at Johnny's—either downtown or on Fulton Avenue—the Velvet Tango Room, the Ferris Steak House
on Detroit Avenue, Jimmy O'Neill's a few doors south of the
Cedar-Lee Theater, the Mad Greek, or of course, Nighttown—
only a scant handful of bars and taverns I have patronized over
the last fifteen years, but joints I've been in more than a few
times. Like Milan Jacovich, a lot of bartenders in town know
my name.

One of the best-kept secrets in Cleveland is a little tavern
on St. Clair Avenue in the east thirties called Jerman's. Mitzi
Jerman, the owner and for most of her life the bartender, too,
is now close to ninety. While her daughter, Susie, has taken
over most of her duties, Mitzi still makes an appearance almost every night to greet her customers and maybe even pour
a beer or two for an eclectic mix of Slovenians, Croatians, artists, television personalities, athletes, wealthy business types
on their way home from a black-tie benefit—and me. She was
actually born in the upstairs apartment over the bar, and lives
there still; her family has owned the bar and the building for
close to a hundred years. My pal Jim Gelarden introduced me
to Jerman's many years ago, and I eventually placed Milan in
there to meet a client in *The Duke of Cleveland*. Mitzi grumbled
that she didn't want her name in any book because it would

bring a lot of strangers to her door, people she didn't even know. Nevertheless, behind the bar she kept a copy of *Duke*, and showed the customers her name and the description of Jerman's so often that the page was nearly ready to fall out. After Mitzi had the bar painted a few years back, the book was put away for safekeeping; otherwise it would still be out behind the bar.

Milan Jacovich doesn't cook very much or very well, though he manages to make himself a Slovenian sausage meal in several books, boiling and then frying them with onions and slathering them with Stadium Mustard. I love sausage, too—Italian, Polish, and Slovenian—but I don't eat it nearly as often as Milan does.

I do, however, plaster spicy Stadium Mustard on almost every sandwich or sausage. It's made locally, and I've sent it all over the country to friends who haven't visited Cleveland in a while and have forgotten how amazing Stadium Mustard is.

By the way, although everyone thinks of sausage as kiel-base or kielbasa, the Slovenians always spell it "klobasa," and so do I in all Milan's adventures. Even a few literary critics have taken me to task for not spelling it "kielbasa," but they're wrong. I'm not.

At one point in my life, for about a twenty-year span, I was one hell of a chef. I first became enamored of authentic Chinese cuisine when I was over in Hong Kong for several months, and when I returned to Los Angeles I taught myself how to cook Chinese. From there I branched out into preparing Indian and Thai cuisine, and eventually began cooking just about everything—except possibly French. For several years my son, Darren, and I shared a house with one of my best friends, Jim Peck and his son, Jim Junior. Jim was a fine chef, too, and we began a culinary rivalry, swapping the set of knives and the chef hat back and forth from one night to the next. We stopped when Jim gained six pounds and I gained eight, but I continued cooking elaborate meals for friends until about ten years ago when it got too time-consuming. I had to decide if I wanted to spend all day shopping, preparing a personal banquet, and cleaning up afterward, or giving that time over to my writing. I chose writing, of course—for the same reason I hired someone to come over and mow my lawn and trim my bushes. Things like that take precious time away from sitting at the computer and composing—which is how I've always made a living.

Milan Jacovich was a military police sergeant in Vietnam, and vaguely alludes to shooting and getting shot at during the war. I'm older than Milan and didn't go near Vietnam, although in my twenties I spent two years fighting the battle of Augusta, Georgia, and learning how to produce television shows through the U.S. Army Signal Corps. I never got shot at, either—and the last time I pulled the trigger of a weapon, I was wearing army fatigues back in the sixties, courtesy of the now-forgotten draft, and I was firing at a target.

I've mentioned Milan's Vietnam experiences in several books, but refrained from having him get much older as the series wore on, even as I aged every day. So I eventually stopped talking about Vietnam because I didn't want to "date" his character. To this day I don't know exactly how old Milan really is, even though his sons have matured over the last thirteen books. All I know is that Milan is somewhere in his middle-to-late forties, and remains there.

You probably don't know exactly how old I am, either, although there are places you could find out if you really want to. My age isn't important, because I don't play basketball for a living. The knees stopped working as well as they used to—but that's all anyone needs to know about my age. I can still write, still laugh, and still be romantic—and therefore I remain younger than springtime.

In my books Milan Jacovich acquires his clients by word of mouth, or else they find him listed in the telephone book. One morning I was stunned when a woman I'd never met before called me and wanted to hire me as an investigator to track down her grown son who'd been missing for several years. She had heard me the day before on the radio, being interviewed by John Lanigan and Jimmy Malone, and apparently wasn't listening too carefully because she thought I was actually a private eye for hire rather than a writer of private eye fiction. It took me about ten minutes to convince her that what I put down on paper all comes from my imagination, and that I was in no way capable of looking for her missing son.

By the way, in the books Milan never refers to himself as a "private detective," because that is a mistake. A detective is an official rank in most police forces all over the country, and even though Milan has a few years as a city cop under his belt, he and I both think of him as an "investigator"—or a "private eye," naturally. And "private eye" or "PI" actually stands for private investigator.

When Milan came back from Vietnam in one piece after that fruitless and deadly war, he joined the Cleveland Police Department, egged on by his best friend since they were both ten years old, Marko Meglich. Marko worked his way up to lieutenant in the homicide division, but Milan was in no way the political animal that his pal was, and after a few years he quit "the job" with the cops and set himself up as private— or what some police officers refer to as a "private star" or a "private tin." He remained best friends with Marko Meglich until the seventh and most tragic book in the series, *The Cleveland Local*. After that, Lieutenant Florence McHargue, an African-American officer, took over homicide, and she and

Milan roughly bucked heads for the next six books. Perhaps if I write another one, I might decide to explore what their problem is with each other.

As a Slovenian, Milan is a Catholic, of course, though he's pretty much fallen away from regular church attendance. I belong to no formal religion of any kind, yet in Cleveland I'm friendly with priests and rabbis and ministers from several faiths. I'm an extremely spiritual man, I suppose, but not even close to being a religious one.

I learned from the "Slovenian" notes Dick Russ sent me back in 1987 that many Slovenian men lose much of their hair early on, so from the beginning I had Milan mention that his hairline was moving north and has been doing so, slowly but regularly, since he was in his early twenties. When I was in my middle twenties I began to go gray, and by the time I was forty my hair was totally white—but I still have it all, even though I'm older than Milan. At least I have *one* jump up on him.

Otherwise I'm in trouble. He is six foot three, and I'm five foot ten. He weighs about forty pounds more than I do—and I'm fighting to lose a few more. He played football in high school and in college; I never played football anywhere besides the vacant lot behind my apartment in Chicago, mostly because I didn't attain my current height until I was about seventeen years old. I was just too damned small to get tackled.

I did volleyball during gym period in school; back then there were no such things after school as "organized sports for children." And I would sometimes get together with a bunch of kids at a park or in a vacant lot—and at least one of us was dragging along a baseball bat and a ball. But participating in active sports competition was never one of my things.

As long as I can remember, I've been impassioned about writing, performing, and music, and since the time I was six years old I have been addicted to book reading. Milan never had time for such frivolous pastimes, sports being his medium for letting off a little steam. His major in college was business and psychology, which is why he's probably a straightforward, deep-thinking guy who has trouble seeing the gray spaces between the black and the white.

After reading even a few of my Milan books you'll notice another aspect of life that he and I don't share at all. He has punched out several bad guys and had a few knockdown and drag-out fights as well. As for me, I haven't hit anyone in anger since I was eleven years old. I've thought about doing so on many occasions since then—but I just took the time to talk myself out of it. You'll find, though, that the fictional Milan, despite the violence and criminality he encounters and must ultimately battle as he cruises the mean streets of Cleveland, is indeed a gentle man. I find myself even gentler.

I decided, though, to share one of my own physical peculiarities with Milan, one I didn't really think about until I'd written almost all of the Jacovich adventures. We both have a space between our two front teeth—largely so we can smile at someone and spit in their eye at the same time.

CHAPTER 8

"Here's to Us. Who's Like Us? Damn Few"

ALTHOUGH CLEVELAND'S PRIVATE eye, Milan Jacovich, had a fleeting conversation in *Full Cleveland* with my other private eye from Los Angeles, Saxon, they never met or worked together in a book even though many readers of both series asked me to put them together. I did not do so, for two reasons.

First of all, they'd have to meet and function someplace neutral, like Omaha, Nebraska, because neither gumshoe is familiar with the other's home turf. If Milan Jacovich, with his decent, polite, sincere Cleveland values and a certain affectionate innocence about him, would show up in Los Angeles, the aggressive sharks that inhabit every part of that city would chew all the flesh from his bones and leave him to fend for himself, defenseless in an unfamiliar setting. And if Saxon ever came to Cleveland and walked into Vuk's Tavern on St. Clair Avenue wearing his expensive and riotously colorful California outfits, his three-figure-priced sunglasses, and his slightly superior Los Angeles attitude, the offended Vuk customers would beat the crap out of him and throw him in the dumpster out in the alley.

One of Milan Jacovich's most endearing character traits, readers often tell me, is his almost blind loyalty to his friends.

I endowed him with this quality before I ever learned it for myself. That's probably because I spent more than a third of my life in Los Angeles. Although the weather is excellent, it doesn't change from one season to the next, and if it does, you can't see it anyway because of the smog. More importantly, Los Angeles is a terrible place in which to have friends—unless you're bulletproof.

Mainly, it's a city of transplants. The only person I know who was actually born in Los Angeles and still lives there is my son, Darren, even though he took some time off to try out the atmosphere in Denver, and even spent a few months here in Cleveland—and it's interesting to note that the North Hollywood Hospital in which he gulped his very first breath has been torn down and replaced by an apartment complex. In Los Angeles they bulldoze everything built before 1963 and put up a strip mall with a Dunkin' Donuts outlet and a Blockbuster video store.

"The business"—which is what everyone calls the entertainment industry—is, by its very nature, a lonely profession. You're surrounded by people, of course—making film or television requires an inordinate amount of warm bodies, most of whom carry clipboards and treat anyone except their superiors like cattle—but the relationships tend to be shallow and temporary.

I spent twenty-four years in Los Angeles, writing and producing and rubbing elbows with big stars who, two weeks later, might be waiting tables in a restaurant—unless they're holding boozy court in every bar in town and wondering why their agent hasn't called them back. Now, having been gone since 1990, I keep in regular touch with only six people I knew there, and three of them are mystery writers who became my friends shortly before I left town.

Angelenos you meet and like and cultivate as friends suddenly decide one morning that "the business" is too much for them to bear any further—too cutthroat, too heartbreaking, too uncertain, too fickle, and more often than one might imagine, not very much fun. So someone you've been seeing several times a week for quite a few years all of a sudden calls you up to say good-bye, leaves town, and goes back to their hometown of Ames, Iowa, or Ishpeming, Michigan, to open a hardware store, and you have to find yourself another friend.

However, if you and your new buddy should discover that you're both in contention for the same job on a movie or TV show, that's the quickest friendship-ender I can think of—except, maybe, the cancellation of a show or the "wrap" of a film, in which people with whom you've worked for ages suddenly scurry away to find a new job and probably a new set of friends.

There's also the Los Angeles mantra you must learn to live with if you hope to survive at all: It's not good enough if I have a three-picture, two-million-dollar deal at 20th Century Fox if you have one, too. But if I have that same deal and you're working in a filling station—*now* I have something to crow about.

As a bred-to-the-bone Midwesterner, I never found that an appealing way in which to live. In all those years I never forgot my Chicago roots and values, and I relearned them very quickly when I moved to Cleveland. People born here tend to stay here, to put down roots and build a life, despite the often-wretched weather and the ill fortunes of our sports teams, and latecomers like me seem to plug into the city's warmth and camaraderie and settle in for the duration, too. I've made many friends here, and kept almost all of them. That's because in Cleveland there are real people.

• • •

I HAD MET Dr. and Mrs. John Hadden briefly on one of my quick trips here from Los Angeles, and we kept in touch over the next few years until I let them know I was moving to the area. They were the first to take me out to a celebratory dinner and welcome me, and Lainie Hadden told me I simply *had* to get to know Kay Williams. Sure enough, a few days later, Mrs. Williams called and invited me to a party; I was later to find out she had several get-togethers a week at her home, and the nights she wasn't hosting a party she was a guest at one.

Kay Williams was eighty-seven years old when I was first invited to her home, and definitely a candidate for one of those *Reader's Digest* "The Most Unforgettable Person I Ever Met" articles. Gracious, well-read, well-informed, and with a wicked sense of humor lurking behind a beautiful elderly lady face, Kay was the widow of a world-famous inventor, and we bonded in friendship on that very first night. Later she introduced me to almost everyone I know in Cleveland. You never knew who might be at one of her frequent parties—concert pianists, European royalty, opera divas, American diplomats, and frequently Dr. Benjamin Spock, along with the cream of Cleveland society and an impressive sprinkling of local artists and musicians.

One afternoon when I'd invited her out to lunch, I found when I arrived to pick her up that she wasn't quite ready yet, so I sat at her magnificent grand piano and started to play— mostly American songbook standards and Broadway show tunes. Kay didn't come downstairs for nearly forty-five minutes, and when she finally did, she explained that even though she was hungry and ready for lunch, she'd been enjoying the music so much from upstairs, she didn't want to interrupt me and spoil it.

We lost her after I'd known her only two years, but not a day passes that I don't miss her.

Kay Williams is one of only three non-family members whose photographs are on display in my living room. The other two are people I met through her.

Louise Ireland Grimes Ireland, lovingly known as "Ligi," was another of our city's great ladies. Like Kay, her dinner parties were real "events," although her guest list was smaller and the conversation more spirited. When in her nineties, she was in a horrendous car accident on I-90 near her exit, Brate-nahl, that smashed most of the bones in her foot. Four days later at her beautiful apartment overlooking Lake Erie, she was hosting a dinner party from a wheelchair, a queen to her very soul. On her ninetieth birthday she piloted a Cleveland Fire Boat across the Cuyahoga. I learned much from Ligi, and from Kay Williams, about the world, and about life.

Helga Sandburg Crile is the daughter of American icon Carl Sandburg and widow of the Cleveland Clinic's most famous physician, Dr. Barney Crile. She is a noted poet and novelist in her own right as well as a musician and singer and painter, and she's terrific in everything she does. She's also quite at ease when speaking out if someone or something rubs her the wrong way. An animal lover with a golden retriever, Charles, Helga is at once as elegant as a dowager empress and as warm and familiar as someone in your own family. I've known her for at least thirteen years. I dedicated the book *The Dutch* to her.

I set the final crisis of *The Dutch* in a deep and quiet flow-ered woodland on Helga's Chardon farm. Helga allowed me to wander all over the place alone one lazy summer day, dictating notes about the farm and the woods into my tape recorder, and at one point I was so deep into the woods that I experienced a momentary panic that I'd never find my way out again.

Helga remains one of my dearest friends. She's never

missed one of my book signings—and I've never missed one of hers. Helga celebrates life with every breath, and everyone who knows her has a permanent invitation to the festivities.

•   •   •

I MET SAM and Maria Miller at Kay Williams' house, too. Sam, whose father drove a horse-drawn truck buying and selling old rags in Cleveland, went on to be magna cum laude at Harvard and is the cochairman of Forest City Enterprises. He's arguably one of the city's most visible and powerful men. I had only just arrived from Southern California and I didn't know him from Adam until that first evening at Kay Williams's house. Graham Grund is another marvelous lady who heads the Access to the Arts program and became friends with me almost immediately, especially when she came to my aid that first night when I dropped my napkin on the floor and a horrendous muscle spasm in my back prevented me from picking it up myself. Graham pointed Sam Miller out across the room and told me that every Sunday morning he would visit all his friends and deliver a yummy sack of fresh bagels to them from Bialy's bakery on Warrensville Road. I had no idea exactly who he was that evening, and in my head I made what I thought was an obvious leap of logic. So when I was finally introduced to him I blurted out, "So I understand you're a baker."

He's evidently forgiven me the faux pas because he has been extraordinarily good to me. Sam has a well-earned tough-guy reputation in business, but he's astonishingly brilliant, and one of the kindest and most devout men I know. I dedicated two of my novels, *The Duke of Cleveland* and *The Cleveland Local* to him, because he is the *real* Duke of Cleveland. His beautiful wife, Maria, among her many other accomplishments, chairs and organizes the Scott Hamilton Cancer Initiative ice-skating gala and dinner each year at Gund Arena and the Renaissance Hotel, and is one of the great hostesses of our time. The two of them set a standard for grace and generosity I wish I could live up to. (When the Rock and Roll Hall of Fame and Museum opened to huge crowds and media coverage from all over the world, Sam, who doesn't like rock and roll at all, mused that someone should have built the rock hall about two hundred feet farther north—i.e., right smack in the middle of Lake Erie.)

Carole Carr is another brilliant party giver. She and her husband, David, host a black-tie Christmas party in December at which you can easily consume enough for ten other people, including a huge table of chocolates I can't keep away from. They also give a mammoth Fourth of July gala at their home each year with astonishing and sumptuous food, rides and clowns for the kids, a band, and David's special hobby, a fireworks display that rivals anything you'll see at any Independence Day celebration, amateur or professional. Bless her, Carole buys tall stacks of my novels to give to friends, and I sometimes enjoy just going to lunch with her in a casual restaurant in the quiet east side suburbs where we can talk. When she generously contributed to the benefit auction for Gilmour Academy, I put her name in one of my books—as a slightly inebriated female lawyer. In real life Carole is neither inebriated nor an attorney, but she teases me about using her name anyway.

• • •

IN MOST OF the novels about Milan Jacovich I have included members of the Italian Mob. I've never met any real ones personally—or if I did, I wasn't aware of it. But among the great

Italians of Cleveland, I've known Nick Orlando Sr. almost since I arrived here, thanks to his receptionist, Traci, whom I first met at a book signing and who told me that both she and her boss were faithful readers, and invited me to his business a few days later to meet him. The head of Cleveland's oldest and largest commercial bakery, Nick informed me he was intrigued by the way I wrote about Italians in my books, even though they were all mobsters. "It's respectful," he said. I was impressed, and was delighted that he "got" it; many readers don't.

Nick is a true gentleman, with two terrific brothers, Sonny and John, and great kids, who all work with him at Orlando Baking Company, one of the oldest in the state and makers and purveyors of some of the best bread anywhere. He's also my source material about all things Italian in Cleveland; a few of my books would never have been written without his input. I dedicated *The Irish Sports Pages* to Nick, and acknowledged my thanks to his uncle Carmen Palumbo, who told me some great stories about the days when he was a small kid and lived close by "Bloody Corners" on East 110th Street and Woodland Avenue, some of which I put in that book as a colorfully helpful look backwards.

And of course, since this is a very small town, Nick Orlando is good friends with good friends of mine, like Sam Miller and Carole and David Carr and even Omar Vizquel.

Omar and his wife were enjoying lunch at a big party at Nick's bakery. I've admired lots of ballplayers in my lifetime, but I thought Omar was special, and so I went up to him to tell him that he was the best shortstop I'd ever seen anywhere, and that I was honored to live in a city in which I could watch him play baseball every night. His lovely wife, Nicole, however, got very excited because she was an avid mystery reader, and thought *I* was the big-deal celebrity. She even called her mother in Seattle on her cell phone that very minute to tell her she'd just met me.

I ran into him again when at a terrific party for the publication of his autobiography. I was impressed by Omar's colorful and breathtaking paintings and his professional-scale skill on the conga drum almost as much as his playing shortstop effortlessly and beautifully on the field. I was actually present one night at the Jake when he hit a grand slam homer against the Seattle Mariners. Omar is currently playing for the San Francisco Giants, but I miss seeing him on the infield at the Jake every night of the season.

Probably my best pal in all of Ohio is Peggy Barnes Szpatura, along with her husband, Neal. She's the friend with whom I share my most personal thoughts and fears, and she knows me better than almost anyone. She combines an intense and all-encompassing spirituality with a no-nonsense practicality, and she's also a marvelous and inventive cook. We used to meet at Nighttown or The Mad Greek for a cocktail a few times a month until we both got too busy to fit that in, and I miss those get-togethers, even though we try to see each other as often as all our schedules will allow. Both Peggy and Neal are dedicated to their houseful of stray cats and dogs, loving each of them as much as if they'd gone out and spent a fortune purchasing them.

When Peggy and Neal got married some years ago, I dragged myself from a sickbed to be at the wedding, surprising everyone who assumed I couldn't even walk. But I would have made it to that wedding if I'd had to be rolled in on a gurney. They are those kind of friends.

Reuben and Dorothy Silver are actors and directors, but saying that is akin to simply observing that Tiger Woods plays golf. They are superb artists; both have given performances on stage here that rival anything I've seen on Broadway, especially the first time I ever saw them work, playing the two leading roles in the Swiss play *The Visit*. Many years ago I wrote a profile of them for *Northern Ohio Live*, and I've loved them ever since. Reuben has a Rabelaisian appetite for good food, and they both have a zest for life and music and art, and of course their first love, the theater, and never miss the season at Stratford and the Shaw Festival and a trip to New York City to see *all* the plays. Dorothy was wonderful in *Driving Miss Daisy* and especially in *Master Class*, and Reuben was perfection, even wearing tons of "fat" body makeup as Falstaff in *The Merry Wives of Windsor*. They don't much care for musicals, which is a pity, because if anyone was *born* to play Tevye and Golde in *Fiddler on the Roof*, it's Reuben and Dorothy Silver. They are intelligent, fearless, and immensely talented people, and our get-togethers are always well laced with laughter.

They also star on a radio show written and produced by Larry Kass, a doctor who is an expert at radio history in his spare time. He and his wife, Sarah, put on the show *live* four times a year on WCLV from their home/studio in Hinckley, one of the most elegant and unique places I've seen anywhere, with a lovely radio museum, a working soda fountain, a stained glass portrait of Sarah in the downstairs bathroom, and a splendid waterfall in the foyer. Friends and fans come to see the broadcast, sit in the audience and laugh and applaud, and listen to the wonderful singers and to Channel 3's longtime commentator on the real folks who live around here, Del Donahoo. We are even enchanted with some of the "celebrity" audience as well. I'm especially thrilled to see Herb Score and his wife, Nancy, joining in; he was the top radio broadcaster for the Indians when I arrived here, and of course I recall his greatness when he was standing on the mound in the old Cleveland Stadium and pitching better than just about any left-hander I remember.

• • •

I'VE "KNOWN" CLEVELAND native Ann Elder for thirty-five years or more. We were youngsters together in Holly-wood—I was a TV writer/producer and she was an entertainer on iconic shows like *Laugh-In* and then a two-time Emmy-winning comedy writer. We rarely saw each other—I was married at the time and she was single, and we ran with different crowds. I never knew way back then that she was a Cleveland native—of course, I knew little about Cleveland at all. But when she moved here permanently seven years ago, she called me, and although we made several ill-fated attempts to get together for lunch, we never seemed able to accomplish it and eventually lost touch.

When Joan Andrews, the producer of Lake Effect Radio, called Ann and asked her to do a weekly radio show of film criticism, Ann suggested that I'd make a good on-air partner, and it's certainly turned out that way for the last year. It's also a good omen for me—Joan gave her production company the same name as one of my Milan Jacovich books.

Our studio and Joan's office is on the second floor of the Arcade, which I wrote about more than fifteen years ago. When we do the show each week, we get to look out through the picture window and get a kick out of the people who pass by. As a matter of fact, one nice lady came up to the window during the broadcast and flashed a homemade sign at me that said "WE (HEART) MILAN." By the time we finished our segment and I wanted to thank her, she was gone.

Well, thanks *now,* ma'am, if you're reading this book.

Ann Elder is excitable and full of energy, and I'm very re-laxed and laid-back— and somehow the contrast works. Our show, *Greenlight Reviews*, is a feisty podcast, and I've never had more fun in my life. We don't rehearse, so there are often surprises in store for both of us. (We're *still* fighting over a Bruce Willis's film made from a novel written by an old friend from Los Angeles, Robert Crais. It's called *Hostage*. I loved it, and she—well, we're still fighting.)

Joan Andrews—short, blonde, and pretty, with major dimples that really showed when her photo graced the cover of *Crain's Cleveland Business*—is one of the most dynamic and hardest-working people I know. She produces and edits our show, and her ambition is to become one of the powerful leaders in radio production, and I'm certain she'll attain it, too. Her husband, Patrick, is a handsome and good-natured former cop who has become a teacher.

I get my share of reader fan mail, I suppose—most of it as e-mail—and while I answer every letter, it is rare that I'll become friends with the sender. The exception is a young man who wrote me from Iraq where he was serving as an army pilot, and when I wrote him back we got into a discussion of the war that led to a correspondence. Robi Yucas is a born Clevelander who wrote to me while he was looking out at a vast and dreary landscape of Iraqi sand every day. He described himself as a black Lithuanian, which completely intrigued me almost as much as his intelligent and well-expressed opinions and his deep thoughts and great moral character. Our budding friendship gave me a chance for a personal connection to American military over in Iraq who live in constant danger. Over the course of many e-mails we discovered that despite a thirty-year age difference between us and a vast diversity of interests—Robi is a dedicated jock bodybuilder who regularly bench-presses 405 astounding pounds and who is in love with flying, while my sole exercise over my lifetime has been climbing on and off bar stools and my passions all involve art, music, theater, and writing—we were a lot alike in many ways.

Robi is back in the states now, living in Orange County,

California. When he visited here in the spring of 2005 were able to spend some time together at an Indians-Yankees game with his mother and one of my most loyal fans, Jessyca Yucas—and the Indians actually won that night. A few days later we shared a dinner at La Dolce Vita on Mayfield and Murray Hill in Little Italy—a restaurant that reminds me more and more of New York and the Italian neighborhood on Bleecker Street. The meal and the conversation lasted much longer than I'm sure the anxious-to-go-home servers would have liked. As far as I'm concerned, Robi has become family.

My best friends in all the world, however, are my children. Valerie Lynn Thompson lives in Aspen and runs her own business. She is very funny, very efficient, and has told me she loves me every time we've ever talked on the phone since she became an adult. My amazing granddaughter, Shea ,lives there, too, of course—talented and sensitive and genuine, and one of the nicest fourteen-year-old teenagers in the world. My only son, Darren Jon, is a dedicated beach dweller and a successful entrepreneur, and a lifelong Southern Californian despite all my efforts to lure him to Cleveland for good.

I've thought that Darren ought to put one of his own adventures between the covers of his own book. He could write about his successes as a professional volleyball player or on an outrigger canoe team. About two years ago—*after* the fact—he informed me that he had quietly slipped away to Spain without telling anyone, and carving a little piece of his own personal history with hundreds of other young men from all over the world, he ran with the bulls through the streets of the city of Pamplona. He even sent me a large photograph of himself near the head of a daredevil crowd, racing about eight feet in front of one of the biggest, meanest bulls I've ever seen. Only having heard about it from the lips of my safe-and-sound son saved me from a genuine heart attack. That photograph is framed and on my mantel, and I'm still waiting for Darren to write his stories and get them published.

He makes his home with his beautiful wife, Anne, a neonatal nurse, just south of Los Angeles, in San Pedro, where their condo overlooks the Pacific Ocean.

I have more fun hanging out with my kids than with anyone, and one of the few major sorrows in my life is that we live so far apart. But I don't ski, and Aspen and its environs are just too froufrou for my taste—and the twenty-four years I spent living and working in Southern California were more than enough, thank you.

The dearest pal and love I've ever known died in January of 2004. He was a thirteen-year-old Russian blue cat named Sonny, and he came to live with me along with my son in the spring of 1995. I explained to Darren that if he wanted to hang out with the media and advertising people, I knew almost all of them. If he wanted to rub elbows with the super rich who attend black-tie benefits every week, it wouldn't be a problem, because many of them are my friends, too. And if he wanted to drink beer and go bowling with the blue-collar ethnics who made up a large part of the Cleveland community, I knew a lot of them, too. Milan Jacovich had turned me on to all of them soon after I'd arrived.

Darren, who never saw the beauty in Cleveland that I did, decided to go back to California, but left Sonny with me "until he could get settled." Another three months went by, and when Darren confessed he was still looking for an apartment and was spending most of his nights sleeping on the sofas of various friends, there was no way I was giving that cat back! I told him he could have Sonny *now*—or he was mine for good and I never wanted to hear about it again.

I've never really been a cat person. During my marriage we had many dogs, cats, birds, and other varieties of living creatures, but they were all "family pets." Sonny was just mine. He was more like a dog than a cat. He came to greet me every time I walked in the door—*every* time—and except for his mandatory two-hour nap on my bed each afternoon, he was never more than six feet away from me at any given moment I was in the house. Whenever I was on the phone he'd always meow as if he wanted to say hello. At least ten times a day he'd be up on my lap or my chest giving nose-butts of love. He used to hang around my neck like an old scarf—especially in the heat of summer—and spent hours on my lap or on my mouse pad while I was working (maybe he thought it had something to do with real mice). He was there for so much of my writing the Milan books that I came to think of him as my muse. My last seven novels were written with Sonny in the room, and although I never gave him a writing credit, I know he helped me because his very presence brought me peace and contentment.

In 2002 he was diagnosed with two different varieties of cancer, shockingly, and given eight weeks to live. Thanks to the creative efforts of Dr. Maren Jennings of the Metropolitan Veterinary Hospital down in Copley, he lived comfortably for another eighteen months, during which he received more love and care than most cats get in nine lifetimes. In his last few weeks he had to fight the inevitable—valiantly and well. He taught me more than any human ever did about love, comfort, and strength. When he finally closed his eyes for the last time—sitting across my lap as I stroked and cherished him when Dr. Jennings gave him his final injection—it wasn't because he ran out of love or courage. He just ran out of gas.

Rest well, gentle friend.

• • •

THIS IS A Cleveland memoir and not a kiss-and-tell confession, and with apologies to all the women I went out with in my early years here and in Los Angeles, I'm sticking to that. Suffice it to say that I came to Cleveland a happy bachelor, and met and dated some terrific people. But no memoir of mine would be complete—nor is my life complete, for that matter—without Holly Ann Albin.

It was love at first sight. Up until that moment in my lifetime, I never knew what being in love was really about.

I was teaching a seminar at a writers' conference in Hudson in February of 1999 when we passed each other in the hallway, and I thought she was one of the most stunning women I'd ever seen. After the conference, when everyone was sitting around drinking coffee—she went to two other workshops and not to mine, damn it!—I sought her out and began talking to her. I think what impressed me about her the most is that she hadn't the vaguest idea who I was. When I invited her to go out to dinner with me sometime, she said, "I don't really date very much," and I replied, "We don't have to pick out furniture—it's just dinner."

Nearly seven years later we've picked out a lot of furniture together, and have built a beautiful life. Don't ask me how we do it. I'm a sloppy Oscar and she is a neatnik Felix. I'm a sports fan and she is totally clueless about football. I'm meat and potatoes and she's vegetables and health foods and soy—but somehow we make it work. In addition to being take-your-breath-away beautiful, with lovely hair down to her waist and blue eyes that I can fall into every time I look at them, and having an editorial mind that has saved me from several writing blunders over the past few years, Holly is the nicest, kindest, bravest, and most courageous person I've ever met, and the influence she's had on me—both as a writer/editor and as a human being—is incalculable. If you look up the word "grace" in the dictionary, you'll find Holly's picture as an illustration.

She's shy, and while I'm almost always sociable and friendly she is very quiet among strangers. It takes a long time to get to know her. But every morning I wake up thankful that she's in my world, grateful for what she's brought to my life. I could write an entire book about her, but that would undoubtedly embarrass her.

I love her, and that's all anyone needs to know.

· · ·

THERE ARE LOTS of other Cleveland buddies that I probably should mention: the dean of Cleveland television, Fred Griffith, and his wife, Linda—she might be one of the world's greatest cooks; her Thanksgiving feasts always kick off the holiday season for us. Fred—as kind and wise and brilliant as he appears on the tube, has spent nearly forty years as a TV host and interviewer, and has talked to everyone from kings and presidents and movie stars to a broken-down mystery writer from Cleveland Heights. He is a real television legend. I keep after him to write *his* memoirs; they'd really be something.

Another of the many good reporters on television here in Cleveland is Leon Bibb. He's a top anchorman and reporter, but he also creates a lot of special stories about people here in the area. He did a television news piece on me about five years ago—and it ran on TV for many months after that. We had lunch together and he confessed to me that in addition to being an anchorman, reporter, and even an actor, he really wanted to take the time to write something.

Some years back there was a young man in one of my classes who impressed me with his ability and dedication despite being only seventeen and still in high school. Young Patrick McMenamin told his father about me, and Michael McMenamin, then the managing partner of Walter and Haverfield, invited me to see his law offices which at the time were in the Terminal Tower and encompassed the fabled Greenbrier Suite, designed by the Van Sweringen brothers. I wound up using that legendary landmark in *The Cleveland Local*, even discussing the famous peregrine falcons, Szell and Zenith, who made their home on its window ledge and raised their babies overlooking Public Square.

The McMenamins—Michael, Carol, and Patrick—have remained my friends ever since. Patrick, I'm proud to say, is all grown up and now an associate producer with John Stossel's unit on ABC's *20-20* and is working on several screenplays. Michael, whose triple passions are Ireland, Winston Churchill, and Europe between the world wars, is busy editing his own historical novel that he and son Patrick cowrote. I've read it—several times, actually, as they refined and polished it—and I think it's pretty damn good. Sexy, too.

I used to be a regular visitor to bars and lounges and taverns. Since coming here, I've pub-crawled with Jim Gelarden, a great scenic artist for films, television, and commercials, to out-of-the-way neighborhood taverns I've written about in the Milan books. He recently pulled up stakes and moved to New Orleans with his wife, Claudia, and I miss their presence and their vitality in Cleveland. I vividly remember a little tavern we visited on the west side named, oddly enough, the Ugly Broad Saloon—except there were no photographs of women of any kind in there, only about fifty photographs of the late, great John Wayne.

My friend Ron Watt, whom I first met at Jim's Steak House, penned his own memoir, *A Love Story for Cleveland*, about five years ago and was kind enough to say a lot of nice things about the Velvet Tango Room, and about me. So I'm returning the favor. He's not only a good friend, an excellent drinking companion, and a noted jazz musician (we both play jazz piano, only he does it better), but he knows how to live life to its fullest. He's also written three novels of his own, and most recently cowrote a funny nonfiction tome about the strange and heartless people who are taking over the business world: *Return of the Body Snatchers*.

He never inspired a book of mine, or even a character, but he's inspired this author's living ten times over. He's one of those people who takes big steps, and I admire the hell out of him.

That I can call these good people my friends would be sufficient, because real friends are difficult to come by. That they have shared with me their stories and memories of the city I write about, have offered me their companionship and their love, and have helped me grow and mature and flower as a person is very special indeed.

Thanks to all of you for having my back.

CHAPTER 9

A Little Glitch

I'VE OFTEN SAID that the fifteen years I've lived in Cleveland have been the best years of my life—personally, professionally, and artistically. I've had more fun here, too, made better friends, and done more exciting things than I ever did in Los Angeles, New York, and Chicago combined.

But nothing is perfect, not even my Cleveland idyll; I did have one little glitch that came along to cast a shadow over everything for a while. It certainly wasn't the city's fault, because it could have happened anywhere—but it was the support of the people of the city and region that got me through it.

First of all, let me say that with the exception of one nasty cold (during the god-awful winter of 2004–2005) and a sinus infection eighteen years ago while I was still living in California, I haven't had so much as a headache since 1978. Sure, at my age it might take me ten minutes or so to get out of bed in the morning, and my back goes out once in a while, but even that hasn't happened in so long that I almost forget about it. Living my particular lifestyle, I don't often aggravate my aching back either. One of the best things about being a writer, according to mystery writer extraordinaire Lawrence Block, is that it requires no heavy lifting.

I suppose, too, that I'm the typical clueless male in that for thirty years of my adult life I never went to the doctor for any reason. I'd had some really dangerous experiences with doctors when I was younger—during one vacation when I was five years old, a physician also visiting the resort hotel in Wawasee, Indiana, pronounced that I had a slight cold and should sit out in the sunshine, when I really happened to be coming down with the measles. Thank God that horrendous day in the sun didn't affect my eyes. After that I've not been anxious to repeat visits to the doctor. Besides, I was as healthy as a horse, and despite my advancing age, I never gave a thought to my physical condition.

Big mistake.

I never dreamed it would be so difficult to write this chapter, but I've started it, and I always try to finish what I start. So here goes.

I am a cancer survivor.

I don't wear that label like a badge of honor, or as anything of which to be ashamed, either. It isn't what defines me in my own mind, and it's not something I even think much about anymore. I don't attend any support groups, and at least half the people who know me are totally unaware of my medical history—or at least they were until they began reading this book. I certainly don't try to hide it, but I usually I don't bother telling anyone about my clinical experience unless the subject happens to arise. It's just something that happened to me one summer.

Anyone who has survived cancer, though, will quickly admit that it changed their life and the most fundamental of their beliefs, and that they never again wake up without murmuring a little sigh of relief. They're just damned glad to be alive for another day, and so am I.

It's no fun being led to the edge of the pit and being forced to look in.

I don't include my Big C story in this memoir for sympathy; I'd rather be roundly insulted than pitied. Besides, I am just fine now, thanks for asking—feeling better than I've felt in years and planning to stick around for a hell of a long time, mainly because I get an examination every year and the problem has never come back.

Knock wood.

I decided to include this anecdote in my memoir because for about a year it was as much a part of my daily life as watching the news or reading the paper or writing another Milan book, and because the months of recovery were so vividly colored by being in Cleveland and being blessed with the support system of good friends who literally kept me alive.

It was in November of 1996 that I started having stomach problems. I didn't worry about it because the first two occasions happened when I was out of town—once while I was attending Bouchercon, a major mystery convention named after famed critic Anthony Boucher, which is held each year in a different city. In 1996 it was staged in Minneapolis, and I remember trying many of the interesting restaurants within walking distance of my hotel, including one Cambodian eatery, which I blamed for my sudden unexpected problems. A few months later I was in one of my favorite towns anywhere, Santa Fe, where I had gone to record an abridged version of *Collision Bend* on audiotape. I'm a real sucker for Southwestern cuisine, having spent many youthful summers in New Mexico—especially for *sopapaillas*, which are rarely served anywhere else in the country. That's when I had my second threatening episode, accompanied by a stomachache worse than any I'd suffered since I was a kid. Both times when the internal problem kicked in, I simply figured I'd been eating too much rich restaurant food and dismissed it from my mind.

Fortunately—or unfortunately, I guess—there wasn't another occurrence for a while. But by the following March I was feeling sick all the time—stomachaches the likes of which I hadn't experienced since I was a kid. I tried to ignore them but they began getting in the way of my life. I'd been named Honorary Guest of Honor at the Cleveland Film Festival's Opening Night Gala, and I felt too lousy to even show up. Then I went to the *Plain Dealer* Spelling Bee for Literacy to benefit Project: LEARN. Helen Moise, who ran the event for the newspaper, took one glance at me and said I looked ghastly, and urged me to go home. But I was stubborn and hung in there—foolishly. I was in such pain that I bombed out in the first round, screwing up a common word I could normally spell in my sleep.

Finally, in May, due to my long-held aversion toward doctors, I decided to consult a Chinese herbalist, who told me within about twenty seconds that there was something wrong with my colon. The witches' brew he gave me to cook and drink managed to stink up my house in a major-league way, and the taste of the resultant tea was pretty grievous. It didn't help the way I was feeling, either.

The next day I had lunch with a friend, Suzanne Welsh, now Suzanne Shoger. She knew that I'd been feeling lousy for a while, observed I was ashen, and told me if I didn't go to a doctor immediately, she'd never speak to me again.

Thus it was I wound up in the emergency room of Meridia South Pointe Hospital the following morning—a Wednesday. I had no doctor of my own, and I knew so many people as friends who worked at the Cleveland Clinic, both as health providers and support workers, that I preferred going elsewhere to take care of the problem. In the ER one of the nurses informed me I probably had appendicitis, which relieved me a little bit. Still they poked me, prodded me, took X-rays, and then put me in one of those horrible hospital johnnies that don't quite close in the back and sent me up to a little room with no magazines or TV, where I lay for several hours on an uncomfortable gurney, my stomach hurting, too chilly to sleep, bored out of my skull, and waiting for news of my fate.

Finally, at about three o'clock in the afternoon, a doctor came in. I don't remember his name, and I'm sure he's turned into a fine physician these eight years later, but at the time he looked as though he'd just gotten out of high school, and he was waving a "surgical consent" form in my face, asking me to sign it so they could do an "exploratory operation" on my abdomen.

That poor young man! I said, "You mean with all the bells and whistles you have in this hospital, you're going to cut me open just to see what's going on?" Then I added a few other things—only two words, actually—which are printable in my gritty detective novels but not in a gentle memoir like this one. He literally backed out of the room and away from my blast of temper as if he were tiptoeing away from a raging tornado.

I lay there, stomach aching, and stewed for a while longer, and was just about to find my clothes and go home, when "Doogie Howser, MD," or whatever the hell his name was, returned with an older man who told me he was the chief of surgery, that the tests and X-rays showed that something inside me had burst, and that if they didn't go in and fix it, I would be dead within five hours.

That didn't leave much time for a second opinion.

I called my best friend, Peggy Szpatura—she was still Peggy Barnes back then but only about three weeks away from her wedding—and told her where I was, what was happening, and to make sure that my children were notified and that poor Sonny would get fed until I got back—or in case I didn't.

I was in surgery an hour later. The man with the scalpel, Dr. Merchant, whom I met while I was being rolled into the OR, explained a few things, trying to soothe me and make me relax a little. When I asked him straight out, "Is it cancer?" he said, "It could be cancer."

Well, hell—I asked, didn't I?

As I was counting backwards from one hundred and feeling the first buzz of the anesthetic, I had several thoughts. The first one—the overwhelming one—was frustration; I'm a writer and I felt I had more things to say, more books to write. I wasn't nearly ready to go anywhere yet. The second was regret that I wouldn't get to say good-bye to my golden children and my glorious granddaughter, who was only six at the time; I felt they were being cheated. I couldn't say good-bye to Sonny, either.

The third thought—the darkest one of all—was that everybody I loved was at least two thousand miles away and whatever I was going to have to face, I'd be facing it all alone.

During the backwards count I don't believe I ever got to ninety.

The next thing I remember was waking up not knowing where I was but feeling someone's hands on and around my face, pressing down on me, and I took a panicked swing and connected with what felt like a jawbone. Despite the physical violence of which I write often in my novels, this was only time since I was eleven that I'd hit someone, and I hereby apologize to the male nurse on the receiving end who was administering the oxygen through a mask held over my nose and mouth. Since I was flat on my back at the time, about thirty minutes post-op, I can't believe the punch had too much juice behind it.

When I finally opened my eyes and focused on my surroundings, Peggy was there at the foot of the bed, along with Dawn Pierce, an ex-girlfriend with whom I've stayed friendly for more than ten years now, and even as lousy as I was feeling—including the astonishing pain of an eleven-inch incision—I experienced a rush of relief. S*omebody* was there to look out for me. The two of them were as caring and kind as anyone could possibly be; between them they got me through the next several weeks. Without them, I'm sure I would have perished, and although I've thanked them privately many times, it isn't untoward to do so again here, publicly.

Dawn even stayed with me my first two nights back home. My house in Cleveland Heights is eighty-five years old, a three-story Cape Cod colonial, and while it has charm and history and beauty behind it, it doesn't have all the amenities of a new home in a far-flung suburb—including air conditioning. It was pretty hot at the end of May, and I chose to stay in the slightly cooler area downstairs, sleeping on the sofa in the sunroom where I had—and still have—my only TV set. The only bathroom in the house is on the second floor, and several times a day I had to negotiate a flight of stairs to get up there—mostly with extreme difficulty. The hospital, worried about my using the stairs at all, had thoughtfully sent a portable toilet home with me, but I never did use it, and even today it is still wrapped up in plastic in the corner of the basement as a quiet reminder to me that there are certain things you simply do *not* do in your living room.

With an eleven-inch incision in my chest and abdomen I didn't get around with much alacrity. The day after I finally came home to embrace Sonny and everything else I'd been missing for nine days, things that were personally *mine,* I was attempting to descend the steps, and Dawn was walking backwards in front of me in case I lost my balance and fell. Having to deal with feelings I wasn't used to and tried to avoid, helplessness and rage overcame me. I started to cry halfway down the stairs, telling her there was no way I could live like this. She assured me that within just a few days I'd be scampering up and down those steps just as I always had, and to allow myself this time to heal and get better, and of course she was right.

Not about the scampering, though; I'm just not the scampering type and never was, even after major abdominal surgery.

It was during the initial period of recovery I learned how many really good friends I had in Cleveland—because they all showed up at my bedside in the hospital to visit me nearly every day. Because of the surgical incision, I could barely move or sit up, and touched as I was, I couldn't help feeling a bit chagrined because my hair hadn't been combed for several days, I had tubes stuck up my nose and in several other places I still shudder to think about, and I'm sure my breath could have stopped a charging rhino in his tracks. Like every other hospital in the world, the first thing South Pointe stole away from me was my dignity.

The one who gave me the most comfort was Neal Szpatura, who was soon to become Peggy's husband. For months I'd planned to attend their wedding and cheer them with a toast; now I wasn't even sure I would make it out the door to my car to be driven to the church by someone else. I recall one afternoon when there must have been at least fifteen visitors in my room and I was fighting hard to stay awake and be polite, and Neal came and sat on the edge of the bed, held my hand, and told me very softly that it was no breach of etiquette to simply go to sleep, that everyone would understand. Neal is a shaman and a healer, and my at-home recovery was greatly accelerated by his quiet kindness.

I was a pretty lousy patient, I'm afraid, but although most of the nurses at Meridia South Pointe seemed very professional, they came across without much warmth or compassion for their patients. Only a few went beyond caregiving to a sort of temporary friendship, including a male nurse who was on duty for several days and who actually made me smile when he came in to take care of me. One nurse—she was in charge of the night shift on my floor and I never saw her unless I leaned my thumb on the call button for at least forty-five minutes until she finally paid attention to me and brought me the cup of ice chips for which I was begging—was so robustly unsympathetic and downright mean that I was sure she must have taken her nurse's training at Auschwitz.

I griped and complained a lot, frustrated beyond imagining by having to stay in bed all day and even more discomfited when they made me get up and walk around the hospital corridor several times a day, taking baby steps to avoid the incision hurting like hell, and pushing a rolling rack beside me with the feeding solution actually plugged into my arm. I even apologized to one doctor I'd snarled at quite savagely, telling him that having to be helped out of bed was particularly galling for me because I was the least dependent man he would ever meet. I thought at the time I was unique, but I know now I wasn't. I was just trying to maintain some semblance of control over my life.

But the first thing you're forced to give up during an overnight hospital stay is control—taken away by everyone from the head doctor who comes in to see you every few days to the nurse's aides who wake you up every two hours, even in the middle of the night, to take your blood pressure and your temperature and to stick a needle in your arm and drain out some blood. Apart from all the other terrible things the hospital staff do to you, they just don't let you sleep!

The second thing you lose the minute you enter the hospital is your dignity, which only *begins* with one of those ghastly looking hospital johnnies that are humiliating to everyone. Years later I found myself sympathizing to the Muslim prisoners kept by the federal government at Guantanamo Prison down in Cuba who, for days on end, were not allowed to go to sleep.

Sam Miller, one of my dearest friends, showed up at my hospital room every morning at about 7 a.m. to ask how I was feeling and then would go out and raise hell with the floor staff in case I had any complaints. The first time I opened my eyes, there he was at the end of the bed, wearing his Bogart-style fedora down over one eye. To begin with, Sam is hawklike and determined, and my first thought was perhaps the Angel of Death had arrived to spirit me away. Instead he actually kickstarted my day each morning with caring, friendship, and concern. He even reported to one of my other friends that I was "a very sick man," and I'm delighted to report, eight years later, that I fooled him on that score.

One morning he sent a Visiting Nurse from outside the hospital to speak to me in my room. She wanted to know how I was doing, when I would be sent home, and whether I would need at-home nursing care for a while. She was asking all sorts of questions about my physical condition, and once again I found myself, through no fault of hers, feeling frustrated and humiliated.

"You're very attractive," I finally said, noting she had no ring on her left hand, "and if I met you at a party somewhere I'd probably be asking for your phone number. Yet here we are together—I haven't shaved for days or even combed my hair, and I probably look like I'm about ninety—and we're talking about diarrhea!"

She laughed and assured me that it was okay because she was "clinical." But it wasn't okay. I loathe being an in-patient at any hospital because the staff, from doctors to nurses to attendants, are all so impersonal—and they strip you of the last vestiges of your pride and self-esteem. I never wanted to spend the night in a hospital again.

I had a roommate, too. In the next bed was an African-American man about my age, but he was in a lot more pain than I was and probably reticent at the best of times, and in the nine days we shared quarters I don't believe he spoke four words to me. I was thankful that he was a baseball fan, and every night we watched the Indians together on TV—in silence.

The plan, I assume, was to keep me prisoner at Meridia South Pointe until my lab tests came back. They can keep a Wal-Mart or a BP station open 24/7, but on Friday afternoon the pathology lab in a hospital shuts down like an Ohio liquor store on Sunday, so I had to stay hospitalized for nine days until Dr. Merchant—my surgeon, whom I had not laid eyes on since the first day after the operation—finally came in with the report. I was so glad to see him, I smiled.

"I have bad news," he said, and I felt the smile dripping off my face like melting ice cream at the top of a cone on a hot summer day. He went on to say that the tumor he'd sliced out of my colon had indeed been malignant, but that the cancer hadn't reached my lymph nodes and they'd gotten it all cleaned up. As relieved as I was, I wondered how he would have started the conversation if it had been *really* bad news and that the lab report he carried in his hand was my death sentence.

Hospitals being the coldly clinical places they've become, I had a different doctor looking at me almost every morning—or at least I *thought* they were physicians. One of them confessed to me, after I had asked an important question and mistakenly addressed him as "doctor," that he was actually a second-year medical student. I told him with all the respect I had left that, no hard feelings, but I had some important questions to ask, and he was to leave my room at once and send in somebody with an MD after his name.

Finally one of them, whose name stitched on his white smock actually assured me that he did possess an MD degree, said, "You're in good shape now; we'd like to send you home tomorrow."

"Tomorrow?" I asked. "If I go home this afternoon instead of tomorrow, will I die?"

The answer was "Of course not," and I said, "Then you get to work on those release papers, because I want the hell out of here *now*!"

He did, too, and I learned another great lesson: Take charge of your own medical treatment and don't believe everything the doctors tell you. Ask questions, and if you don't like the answers you get, ask them again in a different way. Despite what many doctors believe, the pure act of getting through medical school does not deify you and supply you with all the answers. As a matter of fact, I've never heard a doctor with enough guts to say "I don't know," and I'm sure there are volumes that they don't know but will never admit to, either.

The difference between a doctor and a writer is that I wad up my mistakes and throw them in the wastebasket; doctors bury theirs.

My post-op care was given over to Dr. Robert Pelley at the Cleveland Clinic. He was pleasant and friendly even when he suggested that I take six months of chemotherapy just to be on the safe side. After that, he assured me, there was a ninety percent chance I could live another twenty years. He was wearing an extremely ugly tie with the Cleveland Indians logo on it, and I figured he was my kind of guy, doctor or no, so I went along with his suggestion. In approximately twenty subsequent visits over the next five years, he wore that same ghastly tie every time I saw him, and it always made me smile.

You've all heard chemotherapy horror stories so I won't

frighten you with mine, like an acquaintance of mine who called me the night before I was to begin treatment and spent forty-five minutes regaling me with the horrible reactions to chemo some of her friends had experienced, to the point where I was certain I was in for six months of unrelieved agony and disfigurement. By the way, if someone you know is faced with the prospect of chemo, don't do that—don't scare the crap out of them. The idea is frightening enough and the actual experience is no picnic, either. Have a little compassion, and don't make them feel even more degraded and frightened of the prospect than they actually are. Luckily I have a strange sense of humor, so I chose to regard her bizarre phone call as funny rather than unspeakably cruel and thoughtless.

The chemical the oncology clinic used on me was called 5-FU, which seemed a most apropos name. I wasn't in nearly as bad a shape as many other chemotherapy patients, and whenever I showed up for my treatment, five mornings a week out of every month, I was saddened to see other oncology victims in wheelchairs or with hats or scarves covering their heads, obviously fighting bravely and with great spirit. Cancer patients are a testament to the wonder of the human condition. I'm not at all a religious person—a pretty dangerous thing to admit these days, especially where certain righteous politicians and theocrats can hear you—but each time I saw a fellow patient, especially the heartbreakingly beautiful children who were fighting with everything they had to survive for one more day, I murmured a little prayer for them, just in case Someone actually was listening.

While I felt lousy most of the time, I wasn't too sick to function. I could walk, I could drive, and I didn't even change my diet because Dr. Merchant had told me that the way I eat had nothing to do with what had happened to me. Even on my worst chemo reaction days—usually the week after the treatment when the inside of my mouth was too sore to ingest anything except a nutritious liquid milk shake—the urge to get back to the keyboard and write overwhelmed just about everything else.

At least ten different people bought hats for me to cover my hair loss. I had caps from several Major League baseball teams in which I had no interest, and even a floppy straw "Paul Gauguin" hat from the J. Peterman catalog. Fortunately—and I'm knocking wood even as I write these words—I lost only about ten percent of my hair during treatment so that nobody really noticed, and it started to grow back within days of getting off the drug. This was a huge stroke of luck; I'm pretty vain about my hair, mainly because at my age I still have so much of it. It went silver when I was in my thirties and was always a great conversation starter. Now that I'm no longer *prematurely* gray—as a matter of fact I'm pretty close to pure white—I still consider it my best feature. The face is sagging a bit, and there are wrinkles even when I'm not smiling, but the hair goes on forever.

Writing, when it's done properly, is an addiction as potent as those caused by drugs, alcohol, tobacco, or sex, and my long post-op period of enforced idleness when I was simply too sore and too exhausted to sit up straight at the keyboard, worked on me like a heroin jones. My body had fallen apart right in the middle of writing *A Shoot in Cleveland*, and I couldn't wait to get back to it. If the chemo sometimes made me nauseous—or so wiped me out in the middle of the day that I was forced to stop working and lie down—that was a price I was glad to pay for survival and the chance to keep doing what I love.

Five years later, when Dr. Pelley told me I no longer needed regular visits to an oncologist and genially kicked me out of his office and suggested an internal medicine physician to monitor my health, I asked him if he remembered telling me I could live another twenty years after the chemotherapy sessions. Of course he did.

"Well, screw you," I said, "because I'm going to do thirty!"

I figured that will take me through until I'm about ninety years old—but even then, I'm willing to bet I'll still have stories to tell and books to write and won't be too happy about checking out. If I make it to a hundred, Willard Scott of the *Today* show could put my photograph on a jelly jar from Smucker's.

•   •   •

THE FIRST TIME I got myself out of the house to go anywhere besides the hospital, I managed to attend Peggy and Neal's wedding at Trinity Cathedral—just three weeks and three days following my surgery. I'd lost thirty pounds in South Pointe, and had to fumble around in my wardrobe for something decent to wear that would almost fit me. Darren had flown in from California to help out and keep me company, and he was of course invited to the wedding, too. He drove me downtown and helped me practically crawl out of the car without pulling out any stitches.

I hobbled across the parking lot leaning on his arm. When we got to the door of the church, I took a deep breath, stood up as straight as I could, and announced to Darren, "It's *show time!*" Then I walked into that church as if I owned it. Many people already assembled for the ceremony were assuming I was half-dead and in no way capable of coming to the wedding—but I fooled them! I managed to stay around for the reception for a while until time caught up with me. I walked up to Peggy and murmured quietly, "I'm going home."

I remember my first lunch date about five weeks after getting out of the hospital. I was meeting Nick Orlando Sr. because ironically enough the same weekend I was getting carved up at South Pointe, he was in the Cleveland Clinic with his own problems. I told him about the chemo sessions to come and said that I wasn't going to let it alter my life in any way whatsoever—that I'd work around the bad side effects and not stop doing *anything* that I used to do before the surgery.

He told me he admired my courage—and I said, "What courage? My other option is to curl up in the fetal position and wait for the birds to cover me with leaves." And that's another lesson I learned: As long as you're physically able, stay active and engaged and involved in the things that nurture you as a human being. It will hasten your recovery.

Marji Dodrill, who was stricken with cancer shortly after I was, went into rehearsal for a difficult and challenging role in the play *Angels in America* in the Dobama Theatre on Coventry Road in Cleveland Heights just six weeks after *her* surgery, and continued to work acting in plays onstage for at least six years, for as long as she could stand up straight. She never groused about being sick—only about all the things she still had to do. She did most of them. That's why I call her my own personal hero.

For my birthday a few years back Holly reprinted and put inside a wonderful card the final paragraph of author John Steinbeck's third chapter of *The Grapes of Wrath*, one of my favorite novels of all time. That chapter is an amazing mini-story about a tired old turtle trying to cross a dusty and dangerous road in safety that's a metaphor for the tired Joad family, and other families in the novel, or for all of us everywhere who try, and fail, and try again, and eventually manage to get back on our own feet and maybe even plant a seed in the process. Holly gave me the card along with a wooden statue of a turtle, and they will forever be on my mantel to remind me that I'll land on my feet, no matter what. It's more important and personal to me than something like the Hope diamond—and the turtle statue doesn't have to be dusted off nearly as often.

My own scar has faded now—not gone, but no longer the crooked, fiery red, eleven-inch incision that nearly made me faint the first time I took off my shirt and looked in the mirror. A lot of the bad memories of that "medical event" have faded, too, even though I had to stir up most of them to write this chapter. But there is one aftermath of my cancer experience that has hung on for the past eight years and which I'm sure will trouble me forever. It never ceases to surprise me.

I've become extremely emotional. About four months into my recovery and my chemo treatment I was not feeling particularly well and was spending the entire Saturday afternoon on the sofa, watching a college football game. I don't even remember the teams who were playing, but when you're feeling lousy it helps to watch anything on TV with a little color and movement. One of the players suffered an injury. I couldn't tell what was wrong with him or what kind of hurt he'd sustained, but the medics came out on the field with a stretcher, loaded him on it carefully, and carted him away. I have no idea who he was, other than that he was a college kid and therefore young—but I cried on my sofa for twenty minutes for his pain and suffering.

When I was a child I used to laugh at my grandfather, who would cry at Fred MacMurray comedies or at westerns—but I don't find those films amusing anymore. I don't mind watching action movies or thrillers during which Sylvester Stallone or Jet Li blow away a thousand nameless and faceless bad guys on the screen, but I refuse to see a movie in which one of the leading characters withers away from a disease and dies at the end. You couldn't get me to watch *Love Story* or *Brian's Song* again, not even at gunpoint!

I never sing anymore, even though I made a living at it for quite a few years in Los Angeles, because I've started listening to the lyrics of the songs and really understanding the subtext behind them, and most of them make me feel sad to the point where I can't quite get the words out. ("Cleveland Rocks" and "I Can't Get No Satisfaction" are exceptions. I *always* chuckle at them.)

I can't even watch the news most evenings, because each time I hear of a brave young American dying in Iraq over weapons of mass destruction that don't even exist, something in me dies, too. Like the football player from eight years ago, I don't know any of them personally, but they break my heart, because they are all my children.

Yours, too.

Some might say that getting kicked in the butt by cancer has turned me into a weak-kneed wimp, but I don't think so. I prefer thinking it turned a fairly self-centered and egocentric man into someone who can tap into the very real human emotions of compassion and sympathy.

During the whole cancer ordeal I discovered another thing that astonished me: At no time was I ever afraid of dying. It was always my *second* choice, mind you, but the thought of my death didn't really frighten me. Being more or less an agnostic I wasn't looking forward to heaven and angels, nor, as was more likely, fearing an eternity of fire and brimstone—but I figured that whatever was coming next couldn't possibly be as scary as my hospital stay. The day they removed the tubes that were plugged into my side and didn't even tell me how much it would hurt, I'm certain I hit an *E* above high *C* that would have been the envy of any coloratura soprano. So I was scared breathless of being hurt, but not at all in fear of death.

Maybe I summed it up for myself the day after my operation when my daughter, Valerie, called from her home in Colorado, obviously agitated and upset. I told her, "If anything happens to me, I want you to remember that in New York as an actor, in Los Angeles as a producer, and in Cleveland as a novelist, I've had the most interesting life of anybody I've ever met. It hasn't all been great—as a matter of fact some of it has been downright lousy. But it's never been dull. I wouldn't mind an epitaph that says, HE WAS NEVER BORED, which is the truth. So if I don't make it through this, I don't want you to mourn my death; I want you to celebrate my life."

I'm very grateful that, so far, I've been allowed to hang around Cleveland and celebrate it myself.

CHAPTER 10

One Man's Poison

I HAVEN'T DISCUSSED the outdoor joys of Cleveland very much, because I admit to being an indoor guy. Sure, watching the Indians and the Browns under the sky and in the fresh air, or enjoying the performances at Blossom Music Center and the Porthouse Theatre, or the shows and Arts Festival at Cain Park, certainly do get me into the great outdoors enough. So, occasionally, do annual events like Vintage Ohio in Kirtland, showcasing wines grown right here in the state of Ohio, and the Yankee Peddler Arts and Crafts Show in Canal Fulton.

Though I enjoy a nice walk early in the morning when it isn't too hot—or too snowy, you won't ever catch me camping, swimming, skiing, sailing, or hiking. I don't hunt, fish, garden, or watch the birds—and I didn't do any of that stuff back when I was younger and living in California, either. My idea of "roughing it," frankly, is to go away for the weekend and sleep in the Marriott Hotel with the window open. My best times in Greater Cleveland have all been indoors.

Of course, there are many exciting things to do outside in the Cleveland area, and if you're interested I suggest you look them up in a real guidebook. I get weary just thinking about them—but one man's poison, as they say . . .

•   •   •

SOMETIMES I THINK that life on this planet is changing more rapidly than those of us over the age of fifty can handle—maybe I'm just turning into an old curmudgeon like Ed Stahl. Still, there are some subjects that really get under my skin, and I'd like to share them with you as I'm sure that, like me, you have your own little pet peeves.

I know, I know, some probably occur in every residential neighborhood in every city—but I can still complain, can't I?

It irritates me that despite our spending millions of dollars building the Rock Hall in Cleveland, most of the annual rock and roll awards take place elsewhere, like New York or Los Angeles; the singers and musicians who are enshrined in the museum hardly ever bother to show up in our town. Then again, the music composers I would love to meet, like Tchaikovsky, Beethoven, Mahler, and George Gershwin and Irving Berlin, are not expected to personally visit Cleveland these days, either.

Service employees who interact with customers no longer care about *service*. When I was a kid, every store owner and the people they employed treated the customers with politeness and respect, hoping they'll leave smiling and come back another day. Now they glare at you sullenly and hope you never come back to bother them again.

One time I dropped into a local dry cleaners with a perfectly clean, yet wrinkled, pair of slacks, and asked the woman behind the counter if I could wait for them to be pressed. Without looking over her shoulder she said, *"The pressers might not have time to do that right now."* When I quietly suggested she ask them, she rolled her eyes up into her head and sighed, carrying them into the back room as if they weighed a ton. Within three minutes I walked out, pressed pants in hand, and mad as hell.

• • •

IN THE CLEVELAND Heights area, I get a little perturbed when I wake up and see that somebody has carelessly tossed little pieces of trash onto my lawn. Nothing major—just detritus of wrappings from McDonald's or Burger King or Wendy's, or an occasional empty can of ale. Sometimes it's an empty Hostess Twinkie wrapper—a snack I've never touched in my adult life. Most of the junk is tossed there by kids who live in my neighborhood and are just passing by. I'm sure they are great kids who will grow into great adults; I just wish they wouldn't throw their junk onto my grass as they stroll by so I have to go out there and clean it up.

Have you ever booked an airplane flight a month ahead and requested a seat on the aisle or near the window, or in the very front (they call them "bulkhead seats") where no one can lean his or her chair back and smash your knees? Then, when you arrive at the airport, your seat has been changed, usually for some ridiculous reason, like some woman needs that seat for her harp. (That's a true story, by the way—she had bought her precious harp its own ticket—and the only place it would fit was in *my* bulkhead seat.) The person on the phone who sold you the ticket, probably someone in Atlanta or Phoenix, is nowhere to be found.

Don't try to change your flight either. Airlines treat you like a criminal and even charge you hundreds of dollars as a penalty—or a punishment.

When you call a phone company or utility provider on the phone—or almost any large business—you don't get to talk to a person at all, but a recording that tells you how to access another recording—and on and on you go. If you wait long enough, and patiently enough, you get disconnected and have to start the whole process over again.

In the past ten years or so the younger drinkers have gone crazy over flavored martinis—the apple, the pear, the coffee, the sweet and the minty, and all sorts of other concoctions. To be honest with you, I hate them all. I'm old enough, I guess, that my martinis are always plain, made with good gin (I prefer Bombay Sapphire) and just a drop or two of vermouth. The flame-haired Melanie, who was bartending at the Velvet Tango Room when I first met her and then moved on to the elegant bar at chef-owner Marvin Kaplan's One Walnut for a while—I mentioned both of them and the restaurant in the first chapter of *The Irish Sports Pages*—made the best, most authentic, and most delightful martini I've ever tasted. When I build a martini at home, I always add just *one drop* of Scotch to the mixture. I don't even substitute vodka for gin, because that turns it into an entirely different drink. I can't stand the upscale and over-the-top martinis, and I hope some day when the kids get older they'll start drinking the good stuff.

Don't even get me started on cell phones. Just look at the drivers on the street, or even pedestrians; more of them are talking on the phone than watching where they're going. They even talk in doctor's offices, in theaters, and even in church. My car was rear-ended while I was stopped at a red light in front of Lake View Cemetery by a man in a Volkswagen Passat who was too busy chattering on his phone to notice me. I wasn't hurt at all, thank goodness, but secretly amused that there wasn't a single scratch on my bumper, yet the front of his Passat had folded up like an accordion. When his insurance company called me that evening and I mentioned that at the moment of impact he was talking on his cell phone, they said that was all they needed to know.

I certainly don't talk on my phone while driving. I never do unless I have an accident, or breakdown or get stuck in traffic and am going to be very late to wherever I'm headed. Otherwise, no one has my cell phone number—not my children, not Holly, not my friends or my publisher—not *anybody*. And I like it that way.

I understand some physicians need to be on call any time of the day or night. Nearly everyone else with a cell phone glued to their ear pisses me off, because they have no sense of their own or anyone else's privacy, and while they're having that crucial conversation about whether they should order the thin crust or the thick crust for tonight's pizza, they're not relating to the human being right in front of them.

Here are some other small things that bug the heck out of me.

Spitting. It's nauseating when someone in the car in front of me stops for a red light, opens the car door, and spits onto the street. I've noticed this more in Cleveland than anywhere else I've been in the country.

Anyone who calls me "Dude." Call me by my first name (preferred), call me Mr. Roberts if you so choose, or if you're being formal, call me "Sir." But don't call me "Dude" under any circumstances. Milan doesn't like it, either, and chewed out a bartender who called him that in *The Irish Sports Pages*. (Forget about "Buddy," "Ace," and "Pal," too, while you're at it.)

Anyone who wears his baseball cap backwards with the bill hanging down the back of his neck. I'm sorry, but what's the point? Most people trying to look cool end up looking pretty dumb, anyway. If you wear your cap hat backwards, you damn well better be a catcher.

Public Profanity. Hey, I can swear with the best of them, and often do. I just don't do it in public where strangers, women, and children are startled, and I don't do it casually, either.

• • •

I GUESS ONE of the strangest things about me is my acute discomfort with too much fuss or notoriety accorded me here in Cleveland. Fortunately, even though my photograph appears on almost all my books, writers' faces are not as well-known as those of actors or football players or TV personalities, and I don't get recognized that often.

Some years back I was telephoned by a nearby Friends of the Library group to give a talk at one of their meetings. The gentleman who called me said, "I can't believe you actually answered your own phone!" I asked him who he had expected to answer—one of the household staff? The upstairs maid? I don't have any of those, like the billionaire in a film like *Remains of the Day*, because I can't afford them and wouldn't keep them around even if I could. I just consider myself an everyday guy who does what he does on a typewriter or computer fairly well, and that's it.

Another woman recently wrote me an e-mail fan letter, and when I answered it, she shot back with, "Are you really Les Roberts writing me back, or are you a secretary?" I explained that Stephen King and James Patterson had secretaries and personal assistants and press agents and housekeepers and managers, but all I have is a guy who comes over and mows the lawn once a week.

I can't hurl a football sixty yards, I can't hit a baseball out of the park, I haven't discovered a cure for cancer or the common cold, and I don't have a porn video featuring me and some postteen rock diva like Paris Hilton playing all over the Internet. I don't understand the personal interest in me—and yet I'm glad it's there, because if it were not, you wouldn't have purchased this book, and I'd have to write the next one living in a packing crate under a bridge.

Years ago I was at a Christmas party in Pepper Pike where I knew absolutely no one except my date. I struck up a conversation with another guest, an executive with an insurance company, who pressed me about what I did for a living, and when he found out who I was and proudly admitted that he read all my books, I feared he was going to kiss the hem of my garments. The flattery and praise got very thick, and he finally wrung my hand as though it were a handkerchief that had fallen into a puddle and told me it was a *real honor* to meet me. I answered that while I was glad that it was *nice* to meet me, it's a *real honor* to meet someone like Nelson Mandela. The true heroes of this world are not always the ones who get their names in show business gossip columns.

I think America's love affair with celebrities is peculiar even at the best of times. When I lived and worked in Los Angeles, I knew some benevolent individuals who also happened to be big stars. Some of them, like Jack Benny, Nat King Cole, Barbara Stanwyck, and James Garner went through their lives without anyone ever whispering one bad thing about them. But times have changed. Many of today's stars range from being mildly unpleasant to outright rude, and sometimes even to the dangerous and the criminal. Almost every day you can read about some pop figure who was nailed for drug use, fighting, domestic violence, reckless driving, throwing a telephone at somebody, having an affair with their babysitter, or even horrifyingly dangling their one-year-old baby over the railing of a hotel balcony while the press took pictures.

Some of the actors I knew in my Hollywood days took their eccentricities to an extremely unlikable place. I won't mention the names that always remind me of arrogance and thoughtlessness and a complete disregard for "the little people" who work on movie and television crews and make an actor look good far better than the director or the makeup artist can. There is a reason why I hung out with so few actors back then—they were strange and peculiar ducks, even for me.

There's an old story, probably apocryphal, about the actor who meets someone not in "the business" and who talks about himself for two hours, nonstop. Finally he says, "Well, enough about me—let's talk about you now. How did *you* like my last picture?" It's a silly story, but it's true. And I wish I had a dollar for every time I heard a celebrity, when confronted with a waiter or a store clerk, bellow incredulously, "Do you know who I AM?"

The only true and decent Hollywood stars I can think of offhand who are loved by everyone today and who are still alive and well are Lauren Bacall and Tony Bennett—and they're both even older than I am. In fact, after my high school senior prom I went with my date and some classmates to watch Tony, then a brand-new singing sensation, doing a show at the old Edgewater Beach Hotel. I was thrilled because we were *both* in tuxedos.

Most of the "big names" we obsess over are those who have done something wrong, like Joey Buttafuoco or Scott Peterson or O. J. Simpson, or even indulged in something incredibly stupid, like Paris Hilton's home movies or the jerk who deliberately falsified news stories for the *New York Times*, or on a local level Frank Gruttadauria and Jeffrey Johnson, who screwed over other people for money and bribes and wound up taking the rap in prison. The grandmother who's raising seven of her daughter's children on a part-time job and a welfare check or the volunteer who spends forty hours a week and buckets of her own money caring for abandoned and/or abused animals are the real heroes of our world, and they are worth ten of creepy Michael Jackson or steroid-pumped Jason Giambi or Britney Spears or even Cleveland's favorite unwed father, LeBron James. Having talent and God-given abilities in athletics or performance is very nice, and having good looks is lovely, too. Having both of them at the same time is terrific.

But standing up and being a real human being is the only thing that's really important.

I like to call it grace, which has nothing to do with being graceful, thank goodness, because I'm clumsy enough to trip over my own feet. It's a certain something inside that separates a lot of worthwhile people from a few totally clueless ones. It's saying "please" and "thank you," which I would have thought everyone's mother taught them, but apparently not. It's not yammering on your cell phone in public when it annoys and disturbs other people, or even worse *driving* while yammering. It's treating everyone, regardless of who they are, where they were born, or what they do for a living, with the dignity and respect that is accorded a human being. We live in a country that grants us more rights than anywhere else in the world, but those with grace realize that they don't have any more rights than the guy standing next to them just because they happen to have money, or fame, or the ability to score thirty-five points or more every night on the basketball court.

What is "grace," anyway? It's caring. And above all, it's respect.

I don't think I should get any more respect than anyone else—but I *do* firmly believe that everyone, regardless of their station in life, is deserving of that respect and dignity that is naturally due them as a human being. I give it, always, and I fully expect to get it. It has nothing to do with writing books or being on the radio or even once having met Paul Newman. If I installed your new toilet or picked up your trash at the curb I'd be entitled to that same respect, too. It's when I don't get it that I tend to turn a little ugly.

Otherwise, I'm a pussycat.

CHAPTER 11

Food, Glorious Food!

MANY YEARS AGO my former wife, Gail, hearing of my many meals consumed in some of the most elegant or most interesting places around here, observed that when I die, somebody will scatter my ashes all over the finest restaurants in Cleveland.

I don't go out nearly as much as I used to. I finally reached the age where gallivanting around every night—and a lot of days, too—just isn't as exciting as it used to be. I have about two alcoholic drinks a month now, and I remember when I'd have three or four almost every night of the week. As far as eating is concerned, even though I miss the rich and sinful restaurant dinners I used to consume several times a week in the past, I've had to cut back considerably on my gourmandizing.

A few years back at the West Side Market, I ran into one of my favorite bartenders in the middle of the morning, and after a long-time-no-see greeting, he asked me why I rarely come around to his bar anymore. I told him that I'd fallen in true love and finally settled down, and when Holly and I are spending a quiet evening at home it never occurs to us to suddenly get all dressed up and drive somewhere downtown just to *drink*.

Yet, many of my early years in this city, I was pretty good at painting the town red. A lot of those places haven't changed a bit. I ought to tell you about some of them.

First and foremost is Nighttown (also one of Milan Jacovich's favorite haunts), which has been around for several decades. It's just at the top of Cedar Hill in Cleveland Heights, but literally a stone's throw from Cleveland itself. Nighttown is the name of one of the most raucous and depraved neighborhoods in Dublin—that's the one in Ireland, not the one in Ohio. It was used in James Joyce's most famous work, *Ulysses*. Later a stage adaptation, starring Zero Mostel, was called *Ulysses in Nighttown*. (And yes, I read the book many years ago *and* saw the play.)

Nighttown is the quintessential Irish bar now, with solid comfort food dinners, and a culinary specialty called "Dublin Lawyer." With four different dining rooms, a bar, and a recently installed outdoor patio, it is decorated with all sorts of strange and unusual paintings and posters and statuary, and over the bar there is a mounted head of a moose that makes everyone stop the first time they see it and wonder if it's real. The bar is well-stocked with nearly anything you might want to order, but there's no doubt many of the customers will be quaffing a pint of Guinness. The stout is so rich and filling, you'll find after one glassful that you won't even feel like eating a meal for several hours.

In recent years owner Brendan Ring, himself a native Dubliner, has turned Nighttown into one of the finest jazz clubs in America featuring some of the best young and hip artists along with old reliable jazz icons like Ahmad Jamahl. That hasn't slowed down the regulars who are at the bar nearly every evening and hardly care at all about artistic jazz. They are at ease just chatting with one another or making talk with relative strangers who drop in to listen and eat—and drink.

Brendan is a good guy, and always very genial while efficiently running one of the best joints in town.

I've been an aficionado of Chinese food ever since I was a small kid, when the big dishes on the Chinese restaurant menus in America were chop suey, chow mein, and egg foo yong. I still like egg foo yong, especially for breakfast or lunch, but my palate has grown far more sophisticated over the years. Especially now that I'm living in Cleveland.

I've discovered many Chinese restaurants here, including Pearl of the Orient in both its locations on the east and west sides, Hunan on Coventry, which invites many Cleveland Heights residents for both lunch and dinner, the large, busy and exotic Boo Long and Li Wah, and a large contingent of small and imaginative restaurants in the Chinatown area just east of the city.

Ironically, when I found the best Chinese restaurant ever, it was just two blocks from my home. It's a tiny restaurant on Taylor Road called the Sun Luck Garden, owned by a master chef named Annie. Her food is so good that once, in *The Cleveland Local*, I sent Milan Jacovich in there to try my favorite dish, the spicy mussels—when Annie serves them just a few times a year, she calls a small, select group of regular customers to tell them about the upcoming "special" event. I'm proud to be included on that list.

Shortly after that novel was published, Annie blew up the cover and the paragraph about her and her specialty and put it on the front door of the Sun Luck Garden, where it remains to this day. Milan says, in part, that the spicy mussels are so good that he'd like to secretly lick all the sauce off the plate if only everyone else weren't looking. As for myself, I try never to miss those spicy mussels, and Holly always gets the crab Rangoon as an appetizer. Sun Luck is the only Chinese restaurant in which we not only like but really *love* all the home-made desserts.

I fell in love with Mexican food when I spent two summers back in the late 1950s in New Mexico, where I was an acting member of the Taos Encore Theatre in a small town in which most of the restaurants were either Mexican or Southwestern. Taos has grown tremendously since then and is a hugely busy ski resort in the winter, but back then it was a sleepy tourist town with as many art galleries as there are in Beverly Hills and a plethora of restaurants with outstanding food. I continued seeking out Mexican food when I went to New York, and then in California. Since settling in Cleveland I've had many meals at Luchita's, both on the west side and lately at Shaker Square, at Villa y Zapata, on Madison, and at La Fiesta up on Wilson Mills Road. Lopez, right across the street from the Cedar-Lee Theater, is more upscale and the food is creative and festive.

My favorite Mexican restaurant of all in the Greater Cleveland area is Marcelita's, just north of Hudson down in Summit County. Their cooking, in my opinion, is very close to authentic, especially the dark, rich mole sauce on the enchiladas, and if you ever get out there—which I highly recommend—you should also try their creamy, salty poblano soup. Their bar is warm and inviting, sometimes featuring a live and exuberant band, and most nights, especially on Fridays and Saturdays, they are extremely busy. Dating couples, mature marrieds, and families with lots of kids all hang out in the spacious lobby or bar waiting for a table in one of the four lively dining rooms. The food is well worth the wait, and Holly thinks their salsa is the best ever.

So are the margaritas.

Since I was old enough to remember, I always hated eating tomatoes. To this day I won't eat raw tomatoes in a salad or slapped into an otherwise delicious sandwich. However, for some strange reason I adore pasta and other food with sauces *made* with tomatoes, especially the sun-dried variety. That means I love Italian food, in almost every Italian restaurant I've tried. My fourteen-year-old granddaughter, Shea, e-mailed me while vacationing in Italy. She was sitting outside a pub in Tuscany and "had just finished eating the best pizza I've ever had in my *life*". Italian food is terrific, from the simplest peasant food to the most elegant and expensive dinner. In *The Godfather*, one of my top five favorite films, one of the best scenes is when Pete Clemenza (played by Richard Castellano), who is waiting around for his orders to begin a shooting war between the Corleone and the Tattaglia families, takes the time to teach young son Michael (Al Pacino) the proper way to cook spaghetti sauce.

I whip up a pretty good batch of sauce myself.

I've had Italian meals in many restaurants in the Cleveland area over the years, but I always have a gustatory experience dining in Little Italy, which I've written about in almost all of the Milan Jacovich mysteries. A lot of students from Case Western Reserve and University Hospital, the second-largest hospital in Cleveland, have moved into apartments or houses in Little Italy, giving the place an interestingly metropolitan feel. But the Italians are still there, occupying many of the same old houses, and those you'll see on the streets are more colorful than ever. The traffic is congested, and the sidewalks, in all but the worst weather, are even more congested.

Mama Santa's has the best pizza in town—I prefer the thin crust to the thicker Sicilian variety. I'm most comfortable in La Dolce Vita, just across the street on the corner of Mayfield Road and Murray Hill and named after the classic Italian film by Federico Fellini, which translates to "The Sweet Life." It's an old place just dripping with neighborhood atmosphere, with very high ceilings and a gorgeous marble bar that must be over a hundred years old, and the customers are always beautiful and full of zest. Every Monday night, guest opera singers supply gorgeous Italian music to accompany the fine cuisine. The food, according to owner and chef Terry Tarantino, is *rustica*—simple but elegant. My friend David Manocchio, a filmmaker, was directing and starring in an independent film called *Crime Noir* and shot a scene in the movie right in the restaurant. (Terry Tarantino played one of the mobster types.)

A very romantic thing to do, especially when the weather is good, is to sit near a window at La Dolce Vita, or outside at one of the tables on the sidewalk, and watch the crowds of people strolling through Little Italy. Its richness and movable scenery are as intriguing to observe as those of the old Italian neighborhoods in New York and Chicago. Forty years ago and more, Little Italy was a lot tougher and displayed a more aggressive attitude, but now it's a tourist attraction for out-of-towners and residents alike. Twice a year there is an Art Walk—many galleries and studios right there in the neighborhood open their doors, and rarely does anyone visit without carrying home some art treasure.

Right there on Mayfield Road is a beautiful Victorian-furnished restaurant called Guarino's—and you have to try Presti's Bakery with all its divine pastries and creations. They are also right there on Mayfield Road. Presti's moved there several years ago from farther up the street and is now almost next door to the old Holy Rosary Cathedral. Families who have lived two and three generations in the same house in Little Italy still go to Holy Rosary almost every morning.

Don't forget the Baricelli Inn, on Murray Hill Road, one of the most luxurious restaurants in Northeast Ohio; its atmosphere just as posh as its food.

They've built some new and very snazzy condos in Little Italy over what used to be a large and much-needed parking lot. Nice places to live, I'm sure—but I miss parking my car there. One thing Little Italy has never figured out in all these years is parking lots.

When my son, Darren, visited me in 1991, about two months after I made my home here, he was at first stunned by my three-story Cape Cod colonial overlooking the sprawl of Cain Park. Remembering that where he lived in Los Angeles a four-bedroom house cost close to $400,000—even fifteen years ago—he almost fainted, wondering where I'd acquired that much money to buy "an estate." He thought perhaps I'd won the lottery. I didn't have the heart to tell him that back then I'd paid less than $80,000 for my house.

He had another "moment" on that first trip here when, knowing how much he loves Italian food, I drove him down to Little Italy for lunch. Luckily I found a space right on the street, and when he started to get out of the car, he jumped right back in and slammed the door. He'd noticed Presti's Bakery, the old shuttered Mayfield Movie Theatre, and what used to be a pawnshop known as the Brotherhood Loan Company (now an excellent restaurant called Nido Italia, run by another friend, Angelo Sidari), and he'd read about those places in my first two Milan novels about his relationship with the mob connection. Before getting out of the car he asked nervously, "Do these guys know what you *look* like?"

He never realized that all the Italians in Cleveland really like the way I've chosen to write about them. Besides, I'm in the phone book if they ever desire to "sit down" and talk with me.

About a year and a half ago my friends Dorothy and Reuben Silver invited us to lunch to celebrate my birthday. On the phone Reuben jokingly asked if I wanted to go to a Turkish restaurant—and I had seen an ad in the newspaper that morning for a "one of a kind" restaurant that recently opened at Cedar Center. The Anatolia Café is the only Turkish restaurant between here and Columbus. The long narrow dining room is painted a startling orange and dressed with hanging tapestries and Turkish musical instruments. The lamb and chicken dishes are fresh and tasty, always perfectly prepared. The four of us tried their sampler plate of appetizers—a plethora of textures and flavors—and their red lentil soup, which must not be missed. If you choose to finish off with some strong Turkish coffee, make sure you're not planning to retire anytime soon. The service is impeccable and very friendly. Holly and I have visited the Anatolia more often in the past year than any other restaurant in town—and have always left smiling.

I wrote in earlier about Johnny's Bar on Fulton, and have used it in several Milan books. Johnny's Downtown, on West 6th Street, is even more attractive, so fascinating that I set an exciting and suspenseful scene right there for a recent novel, a non-Milan thriller called *Wet Work*. The mysterious and extremely dangerous protagonist is meeting with an Ohio politician in Johnny's, and quickly moves him from the front window overlooking the beautiful Terminal Tower across the street to a private dining room in the back because the politician has been designated for assassination. But you won't be looking over your shoulder for a hired killer, so you'll love eating by a window at Johnny's. And stop into the separate lounge, featuring a high-end bar always crowded with important people as well as tourists and looky-loos—a wonderful place to have a predinner cocktail.

For fine dining, Giovanni's Ristorante in Beachwood is a

world-class eating establishment, the most elegant restaurant in town with the highest ratings from critics. I've used it several times as a setting in the books. The owner, Carl Quagliata, doesn't even seem to mind that in my Milan Jacovich books I turned it into fictional mob boss Don Giancarlo D'Allessandro's favorite restaurant and hangout, even though the godfather's doctors have warned him not to drink so much red wine or consume so much rich food. I describe in detail the gorgeous furnishings and paintings on the walls in Giovanni's when Milan visits the Don there in *The Irish Sports Pages*.

Everybody who can afford it shows up at Giovanni's for a first-class dinner. It's one of my favorite special-occasion restaurants, especially for anniversaries with the woman I love, where we enjoy dazzling food and the type of service you would only expect in London or Paris or Rome. The intimate bar, however, is a meeting place for some of the most interesting people in town, and some of the most glamorous women. You're never at a loss for good conversation in Giovanni's.

In most of the Italian eateries in town, make sure you remember to try one of their big, popular desserts. In *The Godfather*, Clemenza, after stopping at a bakery and then carrying out an assigned mob hit in the car, instructs his driver, "Leave the gun. Take the cannolis." It's one of the most quoted lines from the movie—but cannolis are always superb, even if there's no assassin or "button man" around to suggest them.

There are plenty of other restaurants worth mentioning, of course. I take out-of-town visitors to Frank Sterle's Slovenian Country House on East 55th Street, an eating establishment that represents and illuminates Cleveland. Sokolowski's University Inn, on the near west side, has been operated by the same family since 1923 and now caters to many of the well-to-do business people who find time for lunch by simply driving a few minutes across the Cuyahoga River—the Polish food is hearty and always satisfyingly filling. Shuhei Restaurant of Japan, on Chagrin Boulevard, is my favorite sushi restaurant this side of Los Angeles, but I don't think Milan Jacovich is quite sophisticated enough to try it. He doesn't much like Greek food either, but I do—the Mad Greek, a combination of Greek and Indian cuisines, is just across the street from his fictional apartment, and very close to my real home, too. One night you might catch a guitarist or a belly dancer performing their craft.

Of course there are dozens of clubs all over town that feature rock, hip-hop, and blues. One of the most amazing Cleveland musicians can be heard every week at Fat Fish Blue, a Cajun-style restaurant right downtown that draws enthusiastic crowds to hear him. He is Robert Lockwood Junior, who's somewhere in his eighties now and remains the most stirring blues player I've ever heard since I used to hang out watching the late musical icon Big Bill Broonzy at the College of Complexes bar on Chicago's Near North Side. As a teenager I'd managed to lie my way into the saloon just to hear him and to participate in the back-room one-act plays that showed off all us Chicago would-be actors.

I have a special affinity for Spanish food, served in a romantic atmosphere. Mallorca, which opened in 1997 in a remodeled space in the Warehouse District, provides an arresting Spanish menu, and as a special treat a Portuguese liqueur served on the house after dinner. It's such a unique place. The first time I told Holly I loved her was on our first trip together to Mallorca. I've probably told her several thousand times since, in every location imaginable. She tells me, too.

I could go on for dozens more pages about the fascinating restaurants in the area that have welcomed both me in person and Milan on the page, but there wouldn't be time for me to discuss anything else. Author Laura Taxel's book *Cleveland*

Ethnic Eats gives you an entire volume more than I could—
and despite her constant research for the guide, she and her
photographer-husband Barney don't seem to have gained an
ounce.

I never fell in love with food when I was a kid the way I have
as an adult, because my mother cooked simple meals, and almost all of her food tasted the same. Then, when I was married for twenty years, Gail's routine was to cook everything
until it was hot and brown, and then serve it. It wasn't until
New York, and later Los Angeles, that I accepted the challenge of trying different cuisines and discovering that I liked
most of them. That's when the love affair really began.

That's one more reason that Cleveland and I are a perfect
fit. There are dozens of exotic food venues I haven't mentioned
here—and plenty more I haven't even been to—yet.

CHAPTER 12

When You Haven't
Got Your Gun

MY FATHER WAS my closest pal and ally for the few years
we had together when I was a boy in Chicago. Half a century
later I still remember some of the amusing things he said. One
in particular that sticks in my mind was when he would see
something or someone a little bit unusual or off the beaten
track on State Street, or in a crowd somewhere—like at a professional boxing match or a Cubs game—he'd always remark,
"The funny things you see when you haven't got your gun!"

Ohio, unlike any other state I know, is totally different from
one town or one county to another, and it never disappoints,
no matter where you go.

Seventeen miles east of downtown is one of the most
charming places anywhere in America. Chagrin Falls is delightful to visit any time of the year, and on Main Street the
Chagrin River spills over some spectacular rock mounds—fiz-
zling and bubbling down into a constantly swirling pool until
it continues down the river on its merry way. Even when the
water around it freezes up during the worst part of winter, the
picturesque falls capture the eye and the imagination. I have
often gone there all by myself, just to sit by the falling waters
and quietly think—and maybe dream.

Half a block away, in the middle of the square on Franklin

Street, is a rustic gazebo. I had my photograph taken in that gazebo way back in 1987, and more recently just a year ago. I probably will again.

You'll definitely want to cruise by the homes in Chagrin Falls, from the upscale grand to the small and cozy. Once part of the Western Reserve, the residential areas look more like New England than Midwestern. Right next to the falls is one of the most celebrated shops anywhere in Northeast Ohio. It's called the Popcorn Shop. It's rather cramped for space inside but sells yummy popcorn, candy, and gelato that makes the eyes of children and adults alike glow like Christmas morning. During the summer, visitors from the Greater Cleveland area drop into the Popcorn Shop for an ice-cream cone to slurp at while they walk down the street looking in the windows of the unique shops. The citizens of Chagrin Falls have taken to calling them "cone-lickers."

A similar old New England type town is Hudson, Ohio, south of Cleveland in Summit County, just about forty minutes from where I live. Many of the houses are bigger and more expensive than in Chagrin Falls, and recent commercial retail additions have taken some of the charm away, but Hudson is still a great place to live and visit—including another small treasure trove of a bookstore called The Learned Owl, right on the main drag and run by Liz Murphy and sometimes her golden retriever pal, Maggie.

Because they inspired my imagination, I dispatched PI Milan Jacovich to investigate suspicious people from Chagrin Falls in two different novels, and sent him down to Hudson for dinner and a visit in another book, *The Indian Sign*. In that one he hooked up for a short-term business partnership with a female private eye, a woman I christened Suzanne Davis. I made that name very close to a real-life private investigator I've known for years. Susan Daniels is not only a friend, but when I need advice about how a PI investigation usually works, she's one of the people I always call. Attractive and confident after twelve years on the job, she's a lot more successful in her work than Milan is in his—but unlike Milan, she doesn't get caught up in murders and *never* gets into a fistfight.

Two of my favorite spots are in Amish Country, both colorful and fascinating and yet hushed and sacred, too. Just forty-five minutes from Public Square in Cleveland is the town of Middlefield, about thirty miles east in Geauga County. Lots of Amish folk call this area home, and there is a sizable cheese factory and shop just off the main highway. Recently a Wal-Mart opened in Middlefield, and there are plenty of horse-and-buggy outfits parked in specially marked areas along with the cars and trucks. It's a place where the past and future come together peacefully.

Everett Dodrill, a friend who's been living in Cleveland Heights for several decades, often says that one day he wants to move away to someplace where the county name is easy to pronounce, as opposed to Cuyahoga County (pronounced "Kie-a-HOG-a," not "HOE-ga"). Geauga County isn't much better. While rural and lush, it's pronounced "Jee-AW-ga."

Nearby is the town of Burton, which has an old-fashioned log cabin sugar maple factory right on the town square. Throughout the month of March many places in Burton, including the upstairs fire station, have decadent all-you-can-eat pancake breakfasts. Any other weekend, the family restaurant called Bell's, also at the corner of the square, serves satisfying and fattening breakfasts and lunches, too. There is a Red Maple Inn, a much pricier bed-and-breakfast, within a stone's throw. It's a very romantic getaway—especially in the autumn when the leaves are turning riotously red, yellow, and orange. That's when this whole part of Geauga County comes to life with colors.

In my journeys off the beaten track, I often head south to Holmes County, Ohio. People talk about the Pennsylvania Dutch all the time, but there are more Amish and Mennonites in this part of Ohio than anywhere else in the country, including Pennsylvania, interspersed among a quaint variety of restaurants and furniture, dry goods, and quilt shops.

I learned of Amish Country from Eli Beachy. You might know his name, or at least his work. He is an oral historian, an excellent mystery writer, a public speaker, and a participant almost every other weekend in a re-creation of Civil War battles staged all over the east and Midwest. He also knows everything there is to know about the Amish down in Holmes County, and for some reason they all know about him, too.

He has, I guess you might say, fallen away from the Amish lifestyle, though he wears the long and sometimes wild shaggy beard without a mustache, and bluntly trimmed long hair. He lives in an air-conditioned house down near Chippewa Falls Lake in Medina County, drives a car, smokes cigarettes, watches television, is married to a non-Amish lady (and also an excellent writer) named Sharon, and enjoys the hell out of his life. And he really gets a kick out of making fun of me. I don't know why for sure, but for some reason I let him get away with it. We always have a lot of laughs.

We met at a Lakeland Community College Writing Conference back in 1992, one that was run by the good and generous friend of all writers, the late Lea Leaver Oldham, at which we were both speaking. We've been friends ever since. I'll often get a friendly e-mail insult from him, and whenever a newspaper down in Medina County writes a story about me with a photo accompanying it, Eli sends it along to me—with glasses, a mustache, and a beard carelessly scrawled over my photo with a ballpoint pen.

Eli has taken me through Holmes County and its environs many times with each of my visiting children and with Holly. In addition to pointing out all the sights and telling some rather amusing stories about his former neighbors, he taught me the proper way to greet oncoming buggy drivers as we're approaching in the car. With both hands on the steering wheel, I simply and subtly lift my index finger to say hello; if the man in the front seat of the buggy sees me do so, he'll raise his finger from the grasp of his horse's reins to return the greeting.

Holly and I have grown almost addicted to Holmes County. We always stop at the Ashery Country Store to shop for goodies like homemade chocolates and pasta, crinkly bags full of cashews, peanuts, or almonds, fig, blueberry, or strawberry bars, pretzels and chips, and every loose dried herb I've ever heard of. We always bring carrots to the horses in the adjoining pasture. One white horse had a limp the first time we saw him, and we named him Philip, after the disabled character in Somerset Maugham's *Of Human Bondage*. His friend, brown and slightly clueless, we called Joey after the Matt LeBlanc character from *Friends*, who, like the horse, wasn't too bright. We've bought Amish-crafted beds, chests, and dressers from Kratzer Furniture just off Ohio Route 30 and even an upholstered sofa from Homestead Furniture farther down the road. Homestead Furniture, by the way, has a festival every June in which visitors to the store are treated with homemade ice cream and fresh strawberries. It's so good I'd drive all the way down there just to get a plateful.

Eli also took me to the busy tourist town of Berlin—pronounced with the emphasis on the first syllable, unlike the major city in Germany. It's always bustling with visitors, shoppers, and looky-loos from all over the country, and it's as traffic-choked as downtown Cleveland at rush hour. A real treat is Lehman's Hardware store in Kidron. It's large and welcoming, and stocks products that appeal to both men and women, adults and children alike, including some historical items like a permanent wave machine that's about eighty years old. Outside you'll find an old jail cell—you'll get a kick having your picture taken sitting inside it. What tickles me the most, apart from some old-fashioned cooking tools and pots, are some brand-new refrigerators and ovens and even bathroom facilities that conform to the rules of Amish religious behavior and are not built to be plugged into an electrical outlet or connected to modern-day plumbing.

Amish homes don't have telephones either, but some Amish do feel it's all right to have a makeshift booth on the side of the road, just off their property, where phones *have* been installed. The successful and hardworking Amish businessmen do, on occasion, make or even more often receive calls.

Another Holmes County must-stop is Heini's Cheese Shop just outside Berlin, which is about the size of a supermarket. You can stroll down four long aisles of different kinds and flavors of cheese and take a small cube from each of the "taste-me" trays; I guarantee after that you won't feel like eating lunch. Besides the cheeses there are all sorts of country-made delicacies that you'll never find in your neighborhood megastore. In the back room is a treasure trove of candies, including several flavors of freshly made fudge that could almost make you forget all the cheese you've just sampled. The young girls who work behind the counters and the young men who are visible through the windows of the factory where they actually make the cheese are all Amish in dress and demeanor.

I've driven almost all my out-of-town visitors through Holmes County, both with and without Eli as a guide. When my granddaughter, Shea, daughter, Valerie, and son-in-law, Richard Thompson, were here in 1994, when Shea was just three years old, Eli rode shotgun with us and pointed out all the obscure sites that had stories connected to them, including the painted blue door on the house of a man who he assured us had four eligible unmarried daughters. Shea and Valerie came back several years later and we went on our own, making the trip on a Thursday, when the huge barns in Kidron, just across the street from Lehman's Hardware, stage their weekly auction. All sorts of livestock go up for sale—chickens, rabbits, turkeys, goats, and pigs—as well as fresh vegetable crops, a few huge farm machinery pieces, a parking lot full of odds and ends including hardware tools and kitchen utensils, and a load of delicious-looking breads and cakes the Amish women have baked the night before and brought hoping someone will bid on them. Eli explained to me that those who don't get bids on their baked goods are a tiny minority of Amish women in Holmes County who just don't bake very well.

When my son moved to Cleveland Heights for a few months in 1995 we went again, although he remembered it vividly from his first trip to Ohio five years earlier. Everyone in my family is attracted to the simplicity and appeal of Amish Country.

After visiting the good old hometowns of Winesburg (made famous by legendary Ohio writer Sherwood Anderson), Millersburg (where they held the last public whipping in America back in 1932), and Walnut Creek, our favorite place to eat, which has now become almost a tradition with us, is a small restaurant in the tiny community of Charm, nestled somewhere between Berlin, Millersburg, and God knows where else. It's also called the Homestead, like the furniture store, and if you allow yourself to eat a full meal—after what is often a half hour's wait for a table—and top it off with a superb homemade pie à la mode, I guarantee you'll not even think about having dinner—perhaps not for several days. The first time I was at the Homestead Restaurant with Eli, two Amish girls looked over at us and giggled to each other in German.

Eli said they were impressed that a favorite and famous writer had showed up, letting me feel good for about thirty seconds until he clued me in that they recognized him, not me.

I must tell a slightly naughty story about a time when Eli and I were hanging around outside the Homestead after a huge lunch, back when we had recently met. He was actually teaching me how to stand slump-like and relaxed after the meal as Amish men do. A horse and buggy was clopping down the street—the only main street in Charm—with three lovely teenaged Amish girls aboard. The driver had taken her shoes off while driving the horse, and had dangled her left leg out the side of the carriage. Her long skirt had risen to perhaps an inch above her stockinged knee—not showing nearly as much leg as any gawker would notice on any busy Cleveland street corner in the spring or summertime. Funny how that one forbidden leg hanging out in the breeze—such a carefree action coming from such a buttoned-up society—became one of my most astonishing and exhilarating moments. I've remembered it for thirteen or more years.

Almost every back road you drive on in Holmes County features the homes and workshops of Amish carpenters and furniture makers, where many people stop to place orders. If you're doing business with the German crafters—who invariably think of us non-Amish as "the English"—you must have a lot of patience, because they can't exactly say *when* they'll finish whatever you asked them to build. But it's always worth the wait. When you ask them a question on the street, such as "Do you know where the post office is?" they will slowly and sagely nod; yes, they *do* know, and that's the question you asked so that's the question they answer. It's the Amish way—and a lesson in patience.

We've also been to Hartville several times, both for my book signings and to look around and visit the Hartville Kitchen adjacent to the new flea market. A stop in the candy store right downtown is a must as well, if only to try their rich, delicious fudge. I've also done signings and once a book festival in New Philadelphia and discovered it has one of the most beautiful old courthouses in Ohio—much like the historic courthouse in Painesville, which I wrote about in *The Dutch*. New Philadelphia is where, a few years later, I became totally lost on the city's streets during a pounding rainstorm and drove around for more than an hour, frequently in a circle, trying to find the freeway entrance to I-77.

I did a similar book event in the lovely college town of Granville, down south, and I've been to at least twelve or more of the annual Buckeye Book Fairs in Wooster, a welcoming old town, home to Wooster College and the agricultural division of Ohio State University. It's almost like home to me, too. The fair is an all-day event on the first Saturday in November when nearly two thousand people visit and invariably leave with huge armfuls of books of every kind. You'll find local authors who write about Ohio history, quilting, and children's stories, including a gentleman who had written a nonfiction book about his musical career, and one year sat next to me for the entire Saturday and played the saxophone—right in my ear. I always sign and sell more than a hundred books, and real celebrities like cookbook mavens Fred and Linda Griffith, ex-Browns superstar Jim Brown, former Dodger pitcher Tommy John, and the dean of Washington's elite press corps, Helen Thomas, sell four and five times as many books as I do. Occasionally even Amish readers come by the BBF and get a book or two.

One year I was in the exhibit area, sitting back-to-back with former secretary of state Alexander Haig, who decided he wasn't going to speak to me. I didn't take it personally, as he didn't talk to anyone, shake hands, or even accept a book directly from their hands to his; he had his assistant, who looked like a harried former Marine, take the book from the customer, hand it to Haig to sign, and then give it back to them. Haig, you remember, was in the White House when President Ronald Reagan was shot on the street and announced with great authority, "I am in charge." It happened almost twenty-five years ago, but from his deportment and his attitude, it seems that General Haig still thinks he's in charge—of everything.

My very first year at the Buckeye Book Fair, I was signing my books not too far from Jim Brown, who'd just written an autobiography. I knew him slightly from both our Hollywood days when he was a bona fide movie star and an occasional celebrity guest on *The Hollywood Squares*. That morning, when he actually had a moment to breathe, I walked over and reintroduced myself.

Back in his heyday Brown was as intimidating as anyone I'd ever met, probably because he learned it on the football field and never changed his attitude even when he was a star. But here in Ohio years later, his face lit up with a smile, he gave me a hug, and he even rumpled my hair and commented that it had gone even grayer than when I'd booked him on the show twenty-some years earlier. I was surprised to see him stop and pose for a picture with a fan's little boy.

Finally, a bit stunned by his new, benign personality, I said, "Jim, you didn't go and get mellow on everybody, did you?"

He grinned and explained that when he turned fifty he began looking at the world differently, and that he'd started being kind and considerate to the people he met. Then he leaned that awesome nineteen-inch neck my way and whispered in a low, rumbling voice, "I didn't get *too* mellow, though."

I also went to a book fair about a year ago in a town called Bellevue, west of here and not too far from Norwalk. In addition to being the site of the oldest restaurant in Ohio, it boasts an actual earthquake-type fault that runs beneath the entire city. The main street just west of downtown Bellevue has many beautiful, newly painted old Victorian houses that cause drivers to slow down and gawk. I've also heard whisperings that some of the homes in Bellevue are actually haunted.

It was the town's first book fair and they did fairly well, but the biggest deal about Bellevue, to me anyway, is that one of my dear friends was born and raised there.

Richard Gildenmeister is a true genius when it comes to marketing and selling books. He's been in the business for more than fifty years, working for now-departed stores like Higbee's, Booksellers, and his own shop in Shaker Square, among others. Now he can be found in one of Cleveland's biggest independent stores, Joseph-Beth Booksellers in Legacy Village, where his position is referred to either as "Master Bookseller" or "the Book General." For many years now he's lived a few feet off Shaker Square, and during his career he's met, in addition to hundreds of thousands of readers and customers, virtually every big name in Cleveland. He's been incredibly supportive of me ever since I moved to Cleveland. When I first met him I started calling him "my bookie," and it's stuck.

In many of the places I've been asked to give a talk, Richard Gildenmeister has been there to hype my work and to sell my books afterward. It takes a while to become accustomed to his rapid rhythm of speech, and his handwriting is even more atrocious than mine. He wears colorful and often far-out clothing and accessories, including a dazzling display of bizarre hats and sunglasses—and he's one of the nicest people I've ever met in my life.

A couple of years ago, Holly and I drove an hour or so west

and spent a lovely weekend at a bed-and-breakfast in Grand Rapids. No, not in Grand Rapids, Michigan—Grand Rapids, *Ohio*. In the book *Bed and Breakfast Getaways from Cleveland* by Doris Larson, we read about a restored flour mill, called The Mill House Bed and Breakfast, in that colorful town just thirty minutes south of Toledo. We stayed in a downstairs room that was homey and rustic—full of the most beautiful antique furnishings draped with handmade quilts. We actually considered never leaving. We had a glamorous dinner at a restaurant right down the street, La Roe's, after we had checked out all the antique shops in town. The next morning we were served a delicious breakfast of fresh fruit, granola, sausage, and French toast, cooked by Mill House co-owner Karen Hertzberg, as we looked out across the garden to the canal running alongside the broad river.

Later that day, we enjoyed a canal boat ride, propelled along to the historic lock by a hardworking horse hauling us from the bank. We got a good look at the rapids in the Maumee River, too—but they really weren't as rapid as all that. White-water rafting with my daughter's family on the Roaring Fork River in Colorado—now those are *grand* rapids!

We visited another old town, Zoar, south of Canton—it's also rumored to be haunted, though we didn't have the pleasure of meeting any ghastly apparitions that night. We had both dinner and breakfast in the cozy dining room of the Zoar Inn, right by the river. Many descendants of the Germans who settled in town more than a century ago still live today in the historic old houses that give Zoar part of its unique presence.

Over the last fifteen years I've driven all over the state of Ohio, and Michigan and Indiana, too, giving talks in schools, clubs, and libraries, and have managed to find terrific informal dining establishments in the small towns—in *most* of them, that is. I recall in one little municipality when I asked the local librarian where was the best place to have dinner in the immediate area, she directed me to the East of Chicago Pizza restaurant on the main drag. And even in Toledo—a real city and not a tiny hamlet along a country road—the young woman behind the front desk of the hotel hosting a writer's conference replied when asked the same question that one of the best restaurants in town was the Outback Steakhouse.

When I was in Indianapolis about fourteen years ago at another book signing with my California pal Gar Haywood, we were hankering for steaks and wound up eating for the first time at an Outback there. At the time I had no idea it was part of a vast chain of machine-stamp restaurants that has managed to find itself little toeholds all over America. It's not all that bad, actually, but it has the same look, food, and ambiance from coast to coast. It even has identical cardboard coasters and pushes ordering Foster's Beer.

I need my imagination stirred more than that, even during lunch or dinner.

I make a point of never eating in chain restaurants, never at home and never while I'm out on the road. I once dropped into a nearby fast-food joint to order Cokes for myself and a friend. No food, just two Cokes, mind you—and I asked the server for no ice in one of the cups. I guess I threw her a curve, because she frowned a moment and finally said, "Which one?"

Whether I'm in Ohio, California, New Hampshire, or South Carolina, I've learned it's more fulfilling and enjoyable to find a smaller, independent eatery. In Mansfield, ninety miles south of Cleveland, I discovered an elegant restaurant called Rocky's, right downtown. In Dayton I had the most spectacular steak ever at The Pine Club, which was built fifty years ago when Dwight Eisenhower was president of the United States

and looks as if it's frozen in time; even their efficient wait-
resses of a certain age still wear the hairdos of the 1950s. The
walls and floors are crafted of pine, and the steak I ordered
was so huge and juicy that each side of it slipped off the end
of the plate.

Closer to home in Medina County, with a window overlooking Chippewa Lake and a breathtaking view of the sunset, is
The Oaks. I first had dinner there almost fifteen years ago and
will always remember its lovely rural feel. I was there in the fall
when the large fireplace in the dining room glowed warm and
cozy. Close by is the now-shuttered amusement park in Chippewa Falls, with the skeleton of a roller coaster still visible,
and the boarded-up dancing hall which jumped to the swing
tunes back in the 1940s.

My aversion to the ubiquitous chain restaurants even
traveled with me overseas when I was in Hong Kong writing
a screenplay back in 1977. I was waiting for the elevator at
the Hilton Hotel when a young American couple from Iowa,
waiting with me, were arguing about where to eat lunch and
finally decided on McDonald's. It was none of my business,
but I couldn't keep my mouth shut. I told them that it was
ridiculous to travel nine thousand miles to Asia just to eat a
meal in the same fast-food joint that's right down the street
from their house in Iowa. I talked them into trying their luck
at a Chinese restaurant nearby. When I went in there myself
half an hour later for dim sum, they were in the middle of the
dining room having their lunch and finally looking like happy
tourists. Take a risk—look around and who knows what seren-
dipitous treasures you might discover.

I love going on road trips, seeing quaint old-fashioned Ohio
towns outside of Cuyahoga County and the people who live in
them. As much as I enjoy waking up and writing, there are

times when I *must* take a day or two off and go off on a jour-
ney, taking the time to explore the way Milan Jacovich rarely
has—because unlike him, I don't worry about the funny things
I might see when I haven't got my gun.

CHAPTER 13

Bones to Pick

I'VE WRITTEN AT great length in this memoir about all the things in Cleveland that are extraordinary and that have made me love the city and area I adopted as my own fifteen years ago. I hope that somewhere along the line I've made you smile a little, and maybe even jot down some notes about where you want to visit next.

But there are also things going on in Cleveland that make me outraged, and I can't finish this book without discussing some of them.

The public schools are a total mess, and I'm secretly thankful that my children are far too old to have to go to them. Virtually every school building here is in dire need of repair. Students, who attend classes in dilapidated buildings are hoping for their own personal repair, too, so they can grow up and be effective, concerned citizens. This year the CEO of the Cleveland Board of Education resigned, and I'm hoping whoever is hired to replace her will not receive the superfluous salary that she did—$279,000 annually. Once or twice a year levies are placed on the election ballots, and the Cleveland voters turn them down religiously. The institutions supported by the Board of Education are growing more hungry and desperate for money every semester.

Cleveland is ranked number one in poverty throughout America, or close to it. Most of the citizens who live here are being pushed to the limit, paying some of the highest taxes in the state and in the country, too—and the hardest hit are the homeowners who pay taxes on their property. Several years ago, the Ohio Supreme Court has ruled that the schools are being funded illegally, and that the law must be changed. But for some strange reason, nobody in the legislature has lifted a finger to change it. I have to wonder why this is happening.

I have a lot more steam to blow off concerning the Ohio Legislature and the State Senate, but I promised I wouldn't talk about politics in this book, so I'll keep my mouth shut—for now.

Many years ago, when I'd first arrived here, both sides of the Cuyahoga River downtown, always known as the Flats, were undergoing a tremendous renaissance; the restaurants were either elegant or lively, the bars and dance clubs were hopping—usually excellent places in which to hook up with attractive people of the opposite gender. In the past fifteen years almost all those establishments have closed up or moved away, and the Flats is now much too quiet for anyone seeking a good time and much too dangerous for anyone to visit at night. Today you read newspaper stories about robberies and fights. Parties who drink too much stagger out onto the patio to urinate into the water and fall into the Cuyahoga.

The action in the Flats started cooling off right about the time that the new Waterfront Line of the RTA Rapid was completed, at a cost of millions to the taxpayers. The line now takes riders down to the east bank of the Cuyahoga River to visit what is little more than a ghost town.

Shortly after I arrived here, I was having lunch with a good friend, the late Rod Porter, whose small and elite printing business, Cobham and Hatherton Press, had just published my limited edition Christmas novella, *A Carol for Cleveland*, in which my take on this city was definitely upbeat and loving, even in the midst of the depression of 1991. I asked him whether he knew any people who actually lived right there in town and not in one of the upscale suburbs. He looked appalled and slightly embarrassed and said, "*Nobody* with money actually lives in Cleveland."

It made me think of the stately homes in suburbs like Bratenahl, Shaker Heights, Beachwood, Hunting Valley, and Waite Hills. I couldn't pick out even one mansion in Cleveland proper that is currently an occupied residence. That was a depressing survey for me.

Things change. A lot of ancient buildings in great disrepair in the Warehouse District and on both sides of the Cuyahoga River have now been converted to upscale residential spaces and are occupied by Clevelanders who love the idea of getting out of bed in the morning and simply walking to work.

But downtown Cleveland isn't really conducive to family living. There is only one small chain of supermarkets in the area, Dave's, with a handful of locations. I don't know anyone with children under the age of sixteen who live in the downtown condos, and I think very few people in the wealthier suburbs both east and west have the nerve to venture downtown after dark to embrace the entertainment, the sports, the great restaurants, or just the sparkling ambiance of lights in the city. That's partly because due to recent federal cuts, Cleveland doesn't have enough money to hire a full complement of police officers.

For years politicians and businessmen have been arguing back and forth over building a new convention center here, replacing the far-off and barnlike I-X Center next to Hopkins International Airport. I've tried keeping my mind open to the idea, but after all the backbiting and jealousy going on among the superrich who wouldn't permit a new convention center to be built unless they skimmed off a considerable piece of the financial pie, I just don't care anymore. By the time the convention center eventually earns back the money it will cost to build the thing, no one who remembers how it began in the first place will be alive to enjoy it.

The same thing is going on with the fight to put a gambling casino in Cleveland. Most downstate politicians are dead set against the idea, even though *thousands* of Ohio citizens take vast amounts of their money every weekend and cross the state line to gamble in West Virginia, Kentucky, Michigan, or Pennsylvania. Personally I don't care about casinos, because I never gamble; if it ever gets built I'd probably visit one here in Cleveland just once to see what it's all about, lose about fifty dollars in the slot machines, and never go back again. But more than a thousand jobs would go to our local citizens, and millions of tax dollars would find their way to the city and state treasuries and would do nothing but good for our city's economy. Some of these narrow-minded politicians ought to rethink bringing that kind of money to the state and to the city.

One of the big developers interested in the economic health of Cleveland announced a few months ago that his company will spend over two hundred million dollars to refresh and re-build the Flats, bringing in more top-level condos, and din-ing and entertainment venues, that will once again lure high spenders from all over. But since the big announcement, there hasn't been another word about it—because once more a few of the very rich and very powerful in the Cleveland area won't let it happen unless they get a part of it, and that glorified kickback doesn't include one extra tax dollar that could help the city balance its budget or support its schools and the po-lice and fire departments.

Young people born and raised locally, and who go to school at one of the fine colleges or universities in this state, are bound to make their careers and a decent living as soon as they've graduated by heading to New York, Chicago, Boston, or the west coast. As much as they love the city where they grew up, their chances for ongoing opportunities for advancement here are slim to none. Even ten years ago when I begged my then-twenty-six-year-old son to move here and start over, he only stuck around in the Cleveland area for about five months, becoming frustrated and depressed, and then dashed back to California where he has since flourished.

In 1994 and 1995, when the then-Gund Arena and Jacobs Field and the Rock and Roll Hall of Fame opened their doors, the national media referred to Cleveland as the "Comeback City." After the city had been in the financial and emotional doldrums for thirty years or more, all of a sudden everyone from all over the country was looking at us with approval and pride. Even a good friend of mine from my Chicago youth, Bob Eskin, who visited one weekend and attended an Indians game at the Jake, apologized for taunting me about deciding not to return home to where I grew up but choosing instead to live in "The Mistake on the Lake." He had discovered that Cleveland had finally turned into a vibrant and vital middle western city.

It's ten years later now, and the Gateway area has opened and closed dozens of restaurants and shops, making good money only on the days or evenings of the sports events, and going hungry the rest of the year. The pinnacle on which our status was perched has turned slippery, and, with a bothersome pain in our butts, we've come crashing down into debt, frustration, and the realization that it's not going to get better anytime soon.

The Gund Arena, named after the Gund family who owned the Cavaliers for many years, changed its name to Quicken Loans Arena. The new owner, Dan Gilbert, also owns Quicken

Loans and bought naming rights along with the team. Person-ally I think the new name for our arena sounds totally ridicu-lous. Everyone is hoping we will all begin referring to it simply as "The Q," but it's going to bother me forever. It's also going to be a grotesque name for a venue where some of the finest musicians in the world give their concerts. I can't imagine someone like glorious operatic tenor Luciano Pavarotti sing-ing his heart out at the Quicken Loans Arena.

Mom-and-pop grocery stores, bakeries, independent cloth-ing shops, milliners and tailors, and even most of the sleepy coffee shops serving comfort-food breakfasts and lunches, all but faded into history and some of our memories when the big-time corporations took over and made much of Cleveland look like any other city in America.

There are lots of places, though, that hung on by their fingernails and somehow survived. I try to patronize the old, independent stores and entertainment venues as often as I can, because even though they are vintage and perhaps a bit tired, they recall Cleveland the way it used to be, and in some neighborhoods it still is.

When I came here, the people running this city were movers and shakers, powerful and forward-looking and ready to help. They were all in their fifties and sixties then. Now they are in their seventies and eighties, and as dynamic as they once were, they are also tired. I keep waiting for some eager, suc-cessful dynamo who is thirty or forty years younger than they are to step forward and don the mantle of vision and leader-ship, to build Cleveland up and buff its image once again and then be ready to pass it on, a generation from now, to another group of young lions ready to do the job.

We need new companies, offering opportunities to the peo-ple who've lived here for generations and are so ready to learn "new tricks" and to give back to the community they love.

We desperately need this area, this whole state, to accept with open arms and minds the people who've chosen alternate lifestyles and alternate faiths who flourish in other states but are reluctant to move to Ohio because of small-minded politicians forcing through thoughtless and cruel laws.

We need to throw out so many of the local politicians whose names have been tarnished with mail fraud, bribery, corruption, and scandal—and while we're at it, toss out the so-called businessmen who've actually done the stealing for them, skimming off their percentage before they hand it over.

We need to appreciate the artists who labor here for small profit to make the city and the area look good and feel proud, despite the fact that their dances, plays, books, paintings, and sculpture do not always please the small but vociferous group of Ohio noisemakers who, in the past five years, have drifted away from actual American democracy and turned into a domineering theocracy.

And damn it, we need to be happy!

I've been happy since I moved here one dark and stormy morning, because Cleveland came alive for me just like Paris did for Colette, Moscow did for Leo Tolstoy, and Los Angeles did for Raymond Chandler—all writers whose cities were so ingrained in their psyches that they made the geographical setting an actual character in all their books.

People who've lived here for decades, even generations, revel in the telling and retelling of the stories of their city. They miss the atmosphere of the old days—the stores and butcher shops and produce stands and dairies and bakeries that are now gone, and the beautiful old homes and businesses that fell to the wrecking ball. Missing those old days is good for everyone—but like me, they must look forward to the future. The rest of the country is moving into the rapidly changing twenty-first century. Cleveland has to do that, too, because the future is *today*. It's for you. Enjoy it.

· · ·

I HAD TO sit down and write this memoir about my last fifteen years in Cleveland because they've been the best years of my life, and I wanted to share them with everyone I could. The Greater Cleveland area has more good memories and more happy times for me than anywhere else I've lived in my life.

My years in Los Angeles exceed my years here thus far, and my readers often urge me to write at great length about my Hollywood days. Six of my Saxon mysteries were actually set there, and fans would love to hear all the celebrity stories—the good, the bad and the ugly. Readers now want to read about the real times there, the real celebrities and the beautiful people and some of the dark sides of Los Angeles, too. But as time goes by, my "famous" Hollywood pals fade into obscurity. Younger readers would rather read about the crop of currently famous instead.

So I'm sticking to Cleveland. I've written fiction about it for the last eighteen years and—except for a few random pokes in the eye—that's been working out quite well. I got the idea for the title of this book from one of the great quotable lines in my all-time favorite movie. *Casablanca* reunites former lovers Humphrey Bogart and Ingrid Bergman in the city of Casablanca, in Morocco, at the beginning of World War II. Meeting for the first time in several years following their love affair in Paris, the two go from love to hate and back to love again. When they finally have to part at the end of the film, when Bogart warns Bergman never to forget him. "We'll always have Paris," he tells her.

I love that line as I think most people who've heard it do, too.

Because I've loved Cleveland and its people since I first laid eyes on the city skyline way back in 1987, and because I soon discovered I was truly home to stay, I chose to lift that quote from the Warner Brothers movie classic, play with it just a little bit, and give this personal memoir its name.

The book is for all those who have loved Cleveland for as long as or longer than I have, and also for the newcomers as a welcome and an introduction. Cleveland is a class act—live here, love it, uplift it, and grow with it.